NEVER ALONE

Tapestries of Life

Coping

When Love Isn't Easy

NEVER ALONE

Phyllis Hobe

MACMILLAN PUBLISHING COMPANY · NEW YORK

Macmillan Publishing Company
866 Third Avenue, New York, N.Y. 10022
Collier Macmillan Canada, Inc.

Library of Congress Cataloging-in-Publication Data
Hobe, Phyllis.
Never alone.
1. Solitude—Religious aspects—Christianity.
2. Christian Life—1960–   . 3. Identification
(Religion) I. Title.
BV4509.5.H63 1986   248.8'43'2   86-8469

ISBN 0-02-555910-9

Macmillan books are available at special discounts for bulk purchases
for sales promotion, premiums, fund-raising, or educational use.
For details, contact:

Special Sales Director
Macmillan Publishing Company
866 Third Avenue
New York, N.Y. 10022

10 9 8 7 6 5 4 3 2

Designed by Jack Meserole

Printed in the United States of America

To Geraldine DePaula
for the kind of understanding
that comes from caring

Contents

Acknowledgments

While it is true that each of us has a separate and unique journey to make in the world, it is very important to have good company along parts of the way. I have held onto many strong—yet sometimes trembling—hands; they have made it possible for me to find joy in the journey. I am grateful for this opportunity to give thanks—although I hope those I mention are already aware of my deep gratitude:

To Jay Acton, for his willingness to explore new horizons; to Jean Brodey, for knowing when I needed a lift, and the sensitivity not to insist on it; to Alexia Dorszynski, whose personal courage gave me strength, and whose editorial skills make me happy to be a writer; to Pat Harrington, for combining good business sense with friendship; to my stepfather, Raymond T. Maloy, for the courage to go on without my mother, whom he loved so much; to Judy Mead, for looking life straight in the eye; to Pat and Dick Sternberg, who make me feel like family; to Eleanor Tuttle, for dealing with difficulty so gracefully.

Preface

When we are in the company of others, we find out what kind of person they would like us to be. When we are alone, we find out who we really are.

From the time we are born, we come under many influences. We are members of a family; we are among friends; we are taught how to live in the world; we eventually find a place in it that we call our own. We care and are cared for; we strive and avoid strife; we want and wish for and try to hold on to our dreams. We win some and we lose some; we are given to and taken from. And from all those experiences we gather together the bits of information that form an image of ourselves. In other words, we are what our lives—and our loves—make of us. Or so we think.

But when our lives change—and that is almost unavoidable—does something happen to ourselves as well? Or is there something more enduring in us, something that is beyond the reach of events and circumstances?

In spite of all we have learned in the company of others, we may not yet know who we are. We may know only what others, many of them dearly loved, would prefer us to be. And that may have little or nothing to do with our created selves.

Only God can reveal our identity to us, and He can

do it only in relationship with us. The experience isn't something we can share with anyone else—which is one very good reason for anyone to spend time alone.

Alone is the point at which we leave the influence of others and come under the influence of God. It is the point of collision between the will of the world and the will of God. It is the exact location where we must decide whether we will be of the world—or in it.

We can never be the persons others want us to be. But it is difficult for us to make that discovery when we are in the company of others. We require the sole company of God for us to learn not only who we are, but what we are worth. And we are worth a great deal.

I used to think that alone was a place where you are and no one else is. It isn't. Alone is a world in which you—and I—dwell, regardless of how many other worlds we may enter and leave during a lifetime. It is the unique way that we respond to life—what we value in it, how we pick our way through it, what brings us to tears or gives us pleasure; how much stress we can take, how long we can wait for what we want. Do we bruise easily? If so, do we cover it up with a stretched smile? Or do we shout our anger the moment we feel its heat? Do we reach out to others—or draw them into our lives?

We may not know the answers to these questions, but be assured they are here—within us. And they will go with us wherever we go. Call them characteristics, if you will, but don't treat them lightly. They won't go away, and they won't be changed. They are God's way of explaining us to ourselves.

Alone is always with us. In a sense, it *is* us. It tells us what we need from the world—and what we can give to it. If we are sensitive to its signals, we will find a place where we can feel at home. If not, if we listen instead to the signals of others, we will always feel at least a little lost.

Alone is where we find both comfort and confrontation, both healing and diagnosis of what needs to be healed; being alone protects yet provokes. It is a solitary confinement that is peculiarly blessed. It is where we are admitted to the company of God. And no one else.

Why, then, are we so afraid to be alone? Why do we look upon being alone as the mark of Cain, a symbol that we are unwanted and cast out?

I could say that I wanted to write this book because I learned what it is to be alone. And that would be true.

I could also say that I wanted to assure any men and women who think their lives are over because they are alone that they are mistaken. That, too, would be true.

But there is more.

Somehow, in this crowded world of ours, we have come to the conclusion that there is something wrong with being by oneself. Even those of us who are in the midst of close relationships are considered odd if we require time to ourselves. A few moments of refreshment from a hectic schedule? Of course. Nothing wrong with that. But more than moments? Hours, days, perhaps? Something must be wrong!

Obviously we would find it very hard indeed to deal with Christ Himself who, after being baptized in populated waters in full view of onlookers, then went off into the hills, alone, for forty days and nights. Nor was that the end of it. Throughout His time among us, Christ frequently sought solitude—sometimes so needfully that He physically pushed past the clamors of others to reach it. In a small boat, among trusted friends, He sometimes curled up alone at the farther end. He was not patient with intruders at such moments.

Jesus Christ was not a loner. He enjoyed the company of others and cared very much for His family. He was a popular person, sought after for social gatherings as well as weighty conversations. Yet there were times when He simply had to be alone. And so must we. For the same reasons.

We do not really know who we are until we are alone with God. No one else knows what went into the creation of our unique selves. No one else is familiar with us.

But once we know, we can easily forget, because the world is so ready to redesign us to fit its need and preferences. Discovering ourselves is only the beginning; continuing to be ourselves is something we can't do alone. We need God's help.

There is a big difference between being alone and being lonely. And that is what this book is about. Although I am writing it primarily for women, I intend it for men as well, because we share many of the same problems when it comes to facing life alone after sharing it with others. How each of us got to where we are is not the heart of the book; how we go on is.

NEVER ALONE

1

DOES ANYONE KNOW
YOU'RE HERE?

IT SURPRISES ME that I can relate to a young woman named Allison better than I can to her mother, although I like her mother every bit as much. I'm surprised because Allison is young enough to be my daughter—but the reason we relate so well is that she and I are sharing a similar experience. We are single adult women. I have been married and no longer am. Allison is going on twenty-nine and hasn't yet married. Her mother worries about that. "I don't want Allison to marry just anybody," she says, "but . . ."

She never finishes that sentence, perhaps because she's aware it may not lead to a happy ending. She has seen too many of the other kind. Also, her own husband of many years is seriously ill and she fears that before long she, too, will become a woman alone.

There are many of us. There will be more.

Where did we all come from? From wanting things that didn't happen. And never will.

For instance—

When I Get Married . . .

It is very hard for us to change the way we want life to be. We don't mind adding; it's the subtractions that hurt.

Today's young women are not so different from those of us who are older. When they were not quite steady on their feet, they played house, just as we did. They mimicked the words, phrases, and inflections of parents, brothers, and sisters. They hobbled about in their mothers' shoes and tripped over skirts too long even when hitched up in belts at the waist. They played with makeup and hats and had picnics with their dolls.

They added a few things. They also played at sports only boys were supposed to be able to play, and they played well. They climbed trees without being called silly names; they went out in the rain without catching cold, and it was okay for them to get dirty. They had opinions. They amazed their elders with their ability to study and feel at home with subjects once considered beyond them. Their scholastic grades were important to them because they were going on to college. And on from there to careers. But underneath they assumed what their own mothers—and grandmothers—had assumed: that they would grow up and get married and raise families. Not by giving up their other ambitions and abilities—they would have them, too. It wouldn't be easy. But they were confident they would manage.

Unfortunately, many young women will not get the opportunity to find out whether they can do all the things they are capable of doing. Because women now outnumber men (by almost 8 million in the United States), which means that for many young women today there will not be husbands, homes, and children. It's a cruel subtraction. And it's one that many of us who are older find impossible to accept.

"Why isn't she married?" my stepfather asks me about my friend Allison, who is pretty and caring and capable. He cannot believe that someone with so much to offer may go through life alone.

Many young women have the same difficulty coming to grips with reality. A very talented young woman who is well on her way to a successful career as a designer takes no real pleasure in her achievements because she thinks there is something wrong with her. "Will I ever find a man?" she wonders aloud.

Another young woman is seriously considering marrying a young man she doesn't love, one who is very casual about holding down a job, because "I'm pushing thirty—and I really want to have children."

"I've stopped going to singles' places," Allison tells me. "I'm tired of 'meeting people.' That's all it comes down to—*meeting people*. Hello—good-bye. I want my life to mean more than that." She is starting to do some things that are important to her—going back to school with a more serious purpose, becoming a good tennis player, looking for an apartment to share with a friend.

Don't fault today's young men. They may seem to

be choosy when it comes to getting married, but that isn't the reason why they are reluctant. Many of them, like many young women, are living alone or in temporary relationships. Marriage scares them. Or, rather, it's the end of a marriage that is so ominous.

In other times a young man was urged by his elders to think carefully about the responsibilities involved in getting married. Today that is only step one. Step two is: What will it cost me if the marriage doesn't work?

Steve is a computer salesman. He's thirty-four years old and almost got married—once. "Then I started thinking—I have some friends who are tied up in divorce costs and child-care payments. Those things can go on forever. I don't want to end up like that. And I don't see any marriages that are lasting." He has come up with one possible solution: "Marry a girl who can support herself—in case anything happens."

It Won't Happen to Us . . .

You can feel the shudder that goes through a room when married people learn that married friends are getting a divorce. If it could happen to *them*, well . . .

We would rather believe that divorce happens to mean-spirited people or people who weren't really in love in the first place. We would rather blame divorce on a mistake made earlier in life, a mistake that can be avoided by those of us who know better. But the truth is that some very nice men and women, who seemed to have deep feelings for each other, are finding it impossible to go on living together.

A woman married for thirty-six years is having difficulty thinking of herself as a single person. "I just never expected it would happen to us," she keeps saying. "Not after so many years."

"In our neighborhood, it was like an epidemic," a divorced father of two explains it. "First the couple with the house on the corner, then one in the middle of the block. Finally it hit us." As his grade-school daughter says, matter-of-factly, "All my friends' parents are divorced."

Not all divorced persons remarry. And of those who do, many end up twice divorced. "I still can't think of myself with two former husbands," one woman told me. "That's not the kind of person I am. I grew up expecting to get married—and stay that way. I still wish it could have been like that."

We'll Grow Old Together . . .

There is something different about the way older couples hold hands. It is not with the uncertainty of youth—not with the possibility that the other's fingers, once touched, might pull away; or the giddy sensation if they do not. Men and women who have lived together for many years hold hands with quiet assurance. They know very well the shape of each other's fingers because they have felt—literally—how those fingers have changed over the years. How once-slim,

5

agile hands have stiffened; how the knuckles took on creases; how faint, freckle-looking marks appeared on the skin. They know, too, that the hand reached for will be there, will not pull away. The sensation now is not of giddiness but of comfort, because each is a part of the other, and has been for a long time. The hands coming together unself-consciously is a sign that two lives truly have become one, a rare achievement in our times.

On my way home from the city one day I watched an elderly couple getting off the train ahead of me. He walked a little more slowly than she did, but she shortened her step so that he didn't realize it. At almost the same moment they reached for each other's hand. They reminded me of another couple I knew for several years.

Bob was a pediatrician with a busy practice and Marian, his wife, was also his nurse. Most people envied them because they spent so much time together, but Marian said it wasn't the same as sitting over a cup of coffee at the breakfast table. "We don't have ten minutes to ourselves," she used to say. "But— someday . . ."

Someday Bob would retire. Someday he and Marian would have time to travel. Or to stay home. Either way, it wouldn't matter, as long as they were together.

After Bob retired, he and Marian had a few good years. Then—a massive heart attack, and Bob was gone. "We did so many things together for so long," Marian says, "somehow I thought we would end life in the same way. At the same time. Now I feel as if part of me went with him."

So many older people have the same expectation—and the same disappointment.

I Could Never Live Alone . . .

Those of us who are disconnected—the widowed, the divorced, the not-married—are easy to count because we stand out in a crowd. But there are many others who are alone and we will never know their number because they are always with someone.

It is possible to believe that as long as we are connected to someone, we are not alone. It is possible to tell ourselves that as long as we hear the sound of a key in the door or a familiar footstep, as long as we sit across from someone at a table or sign our Christmas cards with more than just our name alone—we have a relationship. After all, what more do we need?

We need recognition.

Unless we feel that another person knows who we are; unless, when we speak, someone not only hears but understands; unless we are given a chance to meet someone else's need instead of simply taking up space in someone else's schedule, then we are not being recognized as the woman or man we are. And without recognition there can be no relationship. There can only be the worst kind of isolation. Yet the fear of living alone has kept many isolated persons connected for a lifetime.

In our culture we aren't prepared to live by ourselves. It is not considered possible or desirable to be
alone and still survive. Anything is better than that,
and so we put up with abuses and deprivations that are
far more harmful.

Conversation becomes a thing of the past. We stop
using our minds because nobody wants to know what
we think. We demean ourselves by clinging to youth
because we remember that when we were young, at
least somebody *looked* at us. We don't ask for what we
want; we connive to have it offered to us. We have no
sense of possession because nothing belongs to us. We
don't complain, unless we just can't hold it in anymore. But then there's the guilt. We say we won't put
up with the insults. But we do. Or the blows. But
we do. Because on the other side of the door, should
we choose to leave by it, there is no one. And that ter-
rifies us.

We saw this fear of being alone in our young people
who, in their loudly proclaimed freedom and independence, moved in with each other without being married. But after so many of those relationships ended in
pain, our young people are taking another look at being
alone. They are beginning to see it as a valuable part of
life.

Then and Now

When I was growing up, I occasionally saw women
who were alone—widows, solemn women, accorded
dignity. They sat quietly among us, said to be savoring

their memories and waiting to join them. Their lives were clearly over, no matter how much longer they went on.

And, yes, there were those who had been divorced, but very, very few. My mother was one of them, although rather briefly. She married again, as most divorced men and women did, so the divorce counted, but not quite. We didn't always know when divorced people were among us because usually they didn't talk about it. As for those who had not married again, well, apparently they didn't mingle.

Even more rare were those women who did not marry at all. They were said to be waiting for the right man to come along, and when it was past the time when such an event might occur, they were said to have been too fussy. I don't know what they did for social life because they were not particularly welcome among married couples. I remember a past-forty woman who worked with my mother for a time. She was quite pretty, with enormous green eyes and just-graying chestnut hair cut short and curly. She lived with her parents, who were well on in years, but she had her own car and always spent vacations taking a cruise. My mother spoke pityingly of her—"Isn't it a shame, Betty's so lovely!"—and sometimes invited her to visit us on Sunday afternoons. Never for dinner or supper, but always some hour squeezed in between. The two women and I would sit in the living room over coffee and tea while my stepfather worked at his desk in the den. My stepfather made a point of coming out to say hello and shake hands, but he didn't stay. Perhaps he didn't know what to say to a woman who was alone in the world. Perhaps my mother felt more comfortable because he didn't say much.

Some of my teachers had never married, and that was said to be the reason why they were difficult and moody, if they happened to be. Yet some of them seemed to enjoy life, and no one ever attributed that to the fact that they were alone. Single teachers, however, were more acceptable socially, possibly because they seemed to be a part of something, even if it was only the school system.

Many years later, when my own marriage ended, I almost envied the solemn widowed ladies I occasionally saw as a child. At least they had a place in family life. I wondered what would happen to someone who was simply alone—after having been a part of other lives. I did not look forward to finding out.

Eventually I learned that almost everything I assumed about a woman alone was wrong.

For one thing, we are not rare. For another, our aloneness is not always the result of divorce or widowhood. Some of us—many, in fact—are alone by choice. Some of us—many more than I expected—have not married at all, and may never.

We are not, all of us, old or in the middle of life. Many are young. Some of us will not continue to be alone; a surprising number of us will, quite often as a matter of choice. Not that women are deciding against marriage, but rather that we are deciding in favor of a full life—and that may or may not include marriage. We know that one does not guarantee the other.

There have been changes in the way we live, but the way we think is slow to catch up. It still comes as a shock for a woman to find that she is alone—because neither she nor anyone else expects her to be. We still envision ourselves as being in the company of others: young women with their parents, wives with their husbands, widows with their children. Often we cannot see ourselves as being alone even when we are. And some of us always have been, even when we were in the company of others, although we didn't call such times *alone*. We called them "waiting," or "adjusting," or "understanding," even "hoping." We blamed ourselves for being unable to feel as if we had a relationship even when we were with someone.

In Our Separate Ways

Alone is not a time of waiting. It is, or can be, a time of being. Of becoming. When a woman realizes that she is alone, she doesn't stop being a person. She may, however, discover that she has yet to become a full one.

Alone is a challenge. At first, when a woman realizes that there are other women who are alone, she may assume that they are just like her. A woman who joined a support group for single women told me that she wanted "to be with my own kind." A few weeks later she laughed at her own remark. "Who was I kidding?" she said. "Who is 'my kind'? We're all so different!"

Women—men, too—are alone for different reasons,

and the reasons divide as well as console. Divorced women speak harshly about marriage; widows idealize it. From the vantage point of a divorced woman struggling to make a living with limited skills, a widow with even modest means appears to be financially secure. Widows see themselves as victims of tragedy they couldn't avoid; they tend to think that divorced women brought on their own unhappiness.

The younger woman who has not married and who is beginning to consider the possibility that she may not is an outsider in such a group. She knows that marriages end, and so does life, but those aren't the reasons why she is alone. She wants something out of marriage that older women didn't seek because they didn't know they needed it: an appreciation of each other's development as a person, a support for each other's separate efforts to reach goals that may not be similar. Or compatible. Marriage, for these women, is much harder to come by because it demands a great deal more of each partner. It's not surprising that many single young women occasionally suffer deep doubts about the way they have chosen to live. It's never been done before, and not enough time has passed to confirm the soundness of their decision. They may be wrong, they know that. In fact, it is one of their agonies. Enlightened as they are, they realize that life is not something that can be erased and started over again. This is an agony young singles cannot share with women who have already been married, for better or worse. Nor can they fully share the anxiety of an older woman looking for a job she isn't sure she can handle, or the anger of a woman who built her entire existence around someone who isn't here anymore.

Please—Say Something

Whenever it happens, and for whatever reason, when a woman finds herself alone, she feels cut off—not only from the close relationships that once formed her world but, astonishingly, from God. Her spiritual isolation is especially devastating because God was, is, and ought to be constant even when other relationships aren't. If you have ever been in the company of single women, you will hear many topics discussed: money, children, health, who's a good lawyer, how a therapist can help. But little or no talk of God. Even if the women meet in a church they regularly attend.

Part of the problem is that women rarely experience a unique, individual relationship *with* God. Someone else—a parent, a teacher, a husband—is usually a go-between. A woman approaches God like a child, holding on to someone else's hand, being spoken to and speaking through another person. No one ever said this was the way it should be. It simply was. Call it custom, culture, or whatever, it doesn't matter. Or at least it doesn't until a woman discovers that she doesn't even know how God feels about her. All the words she heard through all the other years—the words about unconditional love; about forgiveness; about asking, seeking, knocking; about the comfort only God can give in times of pain, loss, and uncertainty—are they meant for her? If God indeed sets the solitary in families, then what happens to a solitary woman who suddenly has no family? Or to one who has not yet taken her place in a new family of her own? Can they go to God for comfort? For the consolation that all the waiting will lead to something or someone who will make a woman feel like a whole person? Will God listen to such contemporary questions? Will anyone?

Talk to women who have suffered this crisis in their faith and you will find that they also don't have a sense of their own identity. Many have been part of other lives, and when those connections are severed, they don't know who or what they are. Too often, in their panic to become connected again, they rush into disappointing, heartbreaking relationships that bring more pain. Younger women who postpone marriage or decide to remain single wonder if there is any possibility for an identity outside of a committed relationship.

When my marriage ended in divorce, I considered it my own failure. I thought God blamed me, too. I just didn't know how to approach Him in my need for Him. As a woman of faith, I was supposed to stay married. I didn't. How could I explain that to God? What was I to do next? I found all kinds of advice on practical matters. There were good books and wise counselors to assist me with earning a living, keeping my car running, and taking care of my physical health. But inside I still felt isolated. Where was God?—the God I had known ever since childhood. He was gone. He had served the child for as long as she was a child. But I had, in the meantime, become a woman and I had never known God as an adult.

He was there, all right. I just didn't recognize Him. I do now. I have found that the most important connection a woman can make when she finds herself alone is with her own faith. And when I say faith, I mean a sense of the reality of God. Each of us has an identity. Not one that gets rubbed off from our association with others but one that comes forth, slowly, from within ourselves. And the only way we can discover our identity is to experience it through a relationship with the Person who created it. This is something we have to do alone, and unfortunately it may take a crisis in our life to bring us to that brink of discovery. Like Christ, each of us—men as well as women—needs to spend some time alone with God in the wilderness. And, like Him, we will emerge knowing who we are.

Because we don't allow ourselves to learn what aloneness is, we think of it as abandonment. It isn't. Alone is being one-on-one with God. It is the beginning of all relationships between whole, identifiable persons.

When you become alone, your life isn't cut in half. Neither is it over. It changes. You change. You will have to break old habits and even some old relationships. You will have to learn new ways to do things and open yourself to new thoughts, new persons. You will think of yourself in different ways. You are building a new life, not in place of, but *onto*, the life that was, and this is a whole new creation. It's hard work— but worth the effort.

Being alone doesn't mean that you don't see anybody. Or that you don't have relationships. Or love. Or
friends. Or family. You will have all these things, but in
a different way. You might say, in a more realistic way.
In fact, alone is a good place to begin a very full life.

2

EVERYONE'S AFRAID
TO BE ALONE

"I WAS SO AFRAID to be alone," a friend tells me. "I felt as if there was something wrong with me. I mean, if I was alone, it had to be because nobody wanted me. I guess that's silly—but that's how I felt."

No, it isn't silly. It's perfectly human. As long as we continue to believe that life has meaning only when it is shared with someone, I don't think anybody really wants to be alone, at least not for more than a few hours. We begin to feel uneasy. Like my friend, we begin to wonder why no one wants to be with us. There must therefore be something wrong with us. When nobody loves us—

There it is, that word—*loves*. Of course, we're all afraid to be alone, because we associate it with the worst kind of abandonment. If nobody loves us, then we must be unlovable. We feel like infants, not even old enough to sit up by ourselves, our spines not yet strong enough to support us in an upright position. So we lie there helpless, desperately, gratefully dependent on the adults close to us, usually our parents. Being held in the arms of someone strong can end our aloneness, our terror of being abandoned.

17

The feeling persists, doesn't it? Here we are, not only sitting up, but walking around and operating all kinds of mechanical marvels, and we're still afraid that if someone doesn't pick us up and hold us close, we will somehow cease to exist. It's like being convinced that if someone doesn't hold food up to our mouths we will surely starve. We're still afraid of being left in a dark room after someone else has turned out the lights. Or that no one will take us seriously because we're not considered grown up.

A Party of One

They were eight ordinary women. Any one of them might have been your neighbor. And each of them lived alone, for various reasons. The youngest was twenty-eight, and the oldest was seventy-two. Some worked, and some were thinking about getting a job. Some knew each other by sight, and some were strangers, but they all lived in the neighborhood of a large church, which some of them attended. They were meeting together because the church had invited them to share their concerns with one another. The group was led by a young woman with some counseling experience.

At first it was a relief for them to talk about their problems. Until one of them mentioned her reluctance to go anywhere by herself. "The only movies I see are on TV," she said.

The others agreed:

"I'd feel funny sitting in a theater alone."

"I stopped asking my friends to go with me—we don't like the same movies."

"I don't even like to shop alone."

"It's like eating out—which is something else I hardly ever do anymore."

The counselor interrupted. "You mean you've never gone to a restaurant by yourself?" she asked one woman. When the woman solemnly shook her head, the counselor asked each of the others. Same answer.

"Well—that's your assignment for next week," the counselor said enthusiastically. "To go out to dinner—alone."

The response was immediate, unanimous, and horrified.

No, I can't!

I'd be wondering what people were thinking. Why is she here all alone? What's wrong with her?

I'd feel so ashamed. Suppose I saw someone I knew?

The counselor couldn't change their minds, and the meeting ended early. The following week there were so many dropouts that the group was disbanded.

Two of the women kept in touch with each other. They agreed that they ought to do some of the things they felt they couldn't do alone. "We go to dinner sometimes," one of them says. "We take turns choosing the restaurant. Now we both get into the city more often because we go together—and there's so much going on there."

"But we have an understanding," the other one explains. "If something else comes up—well, a date, actually—then we each feel free to cancel our plans."

Sure, It's Scary

Being alone *is* uncomfortable. If you think the women I described were unrealistically anxious, then try walking into a restaurant and asking for a table for one. You will not get a good one—unless, of course, you learn to ask for one. You will be shown to a table set for two, and the second place setting will be whisked away from you as if you might take offense that it was there in the first place. As if it might remind you of better, more companionable times. You will be served quickly, even if solicitously, because what on earth will you do with yourself while you are waiting for your order? By all means bring a magazine or a book to read, if there is sufficient light for such a preoccupation. But count on it—if one other single person, especially one of the opposite sex, walks into the restaurant, he or she will be seated right next to you. Or, better yet, in front of you, so that your eyes must meet at some point during your meal. Both of you are being pitied. Both of you are reminding those around you that they would not want to be sitting in your seat, with your single place setting, with your magazine, with your empty life.

If you can get past that discomfort, you may then become aware of the space you are taking up. You're sitting at a table for two, eating one meal, using a server who could just as easily carry enough for two and thereby make more of a profit for the restaurant. And more of a tip. *Bon appetit!*

For a long time I didn't go to a restaurant alone unless I was in a large city where being the only diner at a table isn't considered unusual. But I enjoyed the experience. As much as I like the company of friends, there is something satisfying about sitting down to a solitary meal—prepared and served by someone else, selected with absolutely no thought about what someone else might choose (and want to share)—without the need to talk or entertain or be interesting. Now that I have learned how to ask for a good table and slow down the service, I find I really need to dine alone as often as I need to dine with friends.

Dining at the home of friends ought to be more comfortable, but it isn't always. You become what my mother used to call "the fifth wheel on the wagon" and no one knows where to put you. You upset seating arrangements unless you bring an escort. Or unless one is provided for you because your friends are convinced that once you meet the right person, your troubles will be over. (And so will theirs.)

Being alone is unfamiliar. Suddenly we realize how many things other people did for us and with us, and we have to learn how to do them by ourselves. Even with small living quarters to maintain, time is gobbled up by all the chores that go into running a home. Unless we pay the bills, get the car inspected, renew subscriptions, stock the cupboard, cook, clean, do the laundry, take out the trash, get to the dentist on time, walk the dog, brush the cat, put money aside for our older years, try to keep up with what is going on in the world, look after our health, keep in touch with our family, and hold down a full-time job—no one else will. Oh, yes, we're supposed to meet new people and join organizations, just in case we don't know what to do with our time.

We can't do it all. We are, after all, only one. And our time and energy stretch only so far. We will not be able to keep up with the laundry the way our mothers did when we lived at home. We may have to send it out. We may have better things to do than mow the grass in a lawn a husband once nurtured. There are such problem-solvers as plumbers, electricians and carpenters. Good friends won't desert you if you don't send a birthday card. If your cupboard is bare, you can eat out or bring a meal in. Some dentists have evening and weekend hours—and not all mechanics are on the other end of town.

You may have to learn how to get help.

Being alone is vulnerable. We get picked on—for the simple reason that there is only one of us, which isn't exactly a formidable deterrent to somebody in a bad mood. Consider Irene, a widow I know who has struggled very hard—and successfully—to bring up her fatherless children in the house they knew as home since they were born. Irene has educated them and watched them depart. She has welcomed them back when they need a rest from the world. She is part owner of a thrift shop that is doing well. She works in a hospital thirty hours a week. Yet when her neighbor objects to her tiny dog walking near the fence that separates their properties, Irene says, "Peace at any price," and calls the dog to the other side of the yard. She changed the location of her washline for the same reason. She cut down a lovely maple tree that the neighbor claimed obscured his view. Irene avoids confrontation because she doesn't feel that is her role in life. That's something for men to do. She is trying to live just as she did when she was a bride, which she refers to often, but without the man in her life. She credits social security—earned by the man who *was* in her life—for making her survival possible. She cannot sense her own strength. And neither can her neighbor.

Being alone makes one feel insignificant. I remember the first Thanksgiving I spent alone. When I looked out my window that evening, I saw that my neighbors' houses were dark. Everyone was away. It wasn't fear that I felt, but something worse. I didn't matter. At least I felt as if I didn't. I couldn't help wondering whether anyone would ever know if anything happened to me. And the logical next question was, Would anyone care? I won't apologize for the fact that I was sorry for myself. I still am, for anyone who suffers that experience. It's not in the mind. It's real.

Being alone is bad for the memory. Because we change what used to be and make it seem better than it was.

A few years ago I was in an automobile accident. Fortunately I wasn't hurt, and neither was the other driver, but our cars were badly damaged. Part of me felt very good because I was able to exchange the necessary information, arrange to have my car repaired, and find a way to get home. Also, I didn't panic. I remembered to call my insurance agent and I had my policy number handy. But I was left with an urgent need to tell somebody what happened. I watched the other driver go to a phone booth on the corner and I imagined him calling his wife, a child, a brother, a sister—someone he could interrupt. Someone who could share his distress and assure him he had done the right thing.

And I knew then that being alone means there isn't anyone you can interrupt. There isn't anyone who can be counted on to drop what he or she is doing and pay attention to what is happening to you. There isn't anyone who can understand exactly how you feel at all times.

Actually, there never was. We only like to think there was, and when we're alone, we forget the many times we tried to share what was going on inside of us and couldn't—because something very important was going on inside the other person as well. Having someone present doesn't mean that that person can always give us what we need.

Perhaps the worst part of being alone is that we feel different. Not the same as other people.

Our lives are less spontaneous. We don't just do something or go somewhere. We consider how long it will take us to get to where we want to go—and how late we will be coming home. We know better than to drive when we're tired, and we hesitate to ask a friend for a lift. That, in fact, is one of our handicaps: we want company, but we don't want to ask for it. So we park in well-lighted areas and we avoid lonely neighborhoods.

We don't like to walk down a street and hear the echo of our own footsteps. No, we're not the only ones to take precautions—but we take more of them.

We also ask ourselves—silently, of course—the same question we dread hearing from anyone else: *Why?*

Why can't I be part of someone else's life?
Why do I have to make it on my own?

One of my friends is as independent as I try to be. But finally we got tired of wondering how we were going to get to the airport, or who could drive us to work when the car broke down, or who might go with us to an event where we didn't know anyone, or who could look after our pets when one or the other of us couldn't. We agreed to call on each other for those favors—and although it has taken some time for us to feel comfortable about it, our lives are a lot less anxious.

You and Your Self-doubt

I can recall the exact moment when I knew I was going to be alone. I lived in a large house at the time, and I knew I wouldn't stay there. It wasn't practical. So I walked through the rooms, running my hand along the backs of favorite chairs, blowing the dust off a tabletop that had already been dusted, putting a book back in its place on a shelf, straightening a window shade, frowning at the third-floor bathroom—a monstrosity, actually, that had been promised a renovation. I was imagining how it would be to say good-bye to the life I knew and to the self I thought was me. I felt apologetic for all the things that hadn't been done, for all the time that had finally run out. I felt as if the house resented me for not doing everything I had hoped to do, and that my approaching aloneness was some kind of punishment.

I had my share of resentment, too. I wanted the house to hold on to me, to keep me where I belonged.

Practically, I had to think about where I would go and what I would take with me. But that wasn't what was bothering me. I was worried about the way people would regard me. Not the way they would address me on envelopes—there are rules for such things. But what place would they assign me in their lives? What would they need that I could give so that I might still be a part of them? Would we talk about the same things? Would we go to the same places we once enjoyed? Would they stop telling me about some events in their lives because they thought I wasn't interested or would no longer understand? Would I find anything interesting to tell them?

Or would they greet me coolly, their eyes asking, Who are you? And what are you doing here?

No one ever actually asked me those questions. I know now that I was asking them of myself.

For most of my life I assumed that I was here to love and be loved. I assumed that I was born of the love of two people and that my life would resemble theirs. When it became obvious that the two people did not love each other anymore, my expectations didn't change. People make mistakes, I concluded, but the purpose of life remains the same.

When I—and many others I knew—made the same mistakes our parents had made, I felt as if I had been deceived. I was reminded of my childhood passion for fairy tales—and the sick feeling in the pit of my stomach when I found out they weren't true to life. I was angry at my parents, angry at the librarian who recommended the books, angry at everyone who had promised me something that didn't exist: a sense of belonging.

It was a long time before I realized that all the myths and all the promises were honestly given to me by people, just like me, who wanted to believe they were true. By people—again, like me—who would rather blame themselves for failure than consider the possibility that the myth was wrong to begin with. Because once we give up the myth, what *do* we have?

Please Take Note

Being alone does not mean that you are a misfit. Or rejected. Or unwanted. Your longing for relationship is perfectly normal.

What makes you feel different is that you are faced with certain realities that all of us can avoid as long as we are in the company of others. You're asking yourself, *Can I love?* and *Can I be?* Things you always used to take for granted.

We grew up assuming that loving and being were

the same. That once we were loved, we would become whole. That once we belonged to someone, our lives would have purpose. We would be happy. There would be no need to ask questions.

Now, we still want to be happy. We still want love and we want life to have meaning. But—how?

The only good thing about being alone is that it is where God can get at us. It is where He can show us that we are no longer helpless. That we can feed ourselves. And if we don't like being in the dark, we can turn on the light—and leave it on until morning if we choose. Yes, *choose*. Another important word. It means that we are living in the now, not in the poorly remembered past. It means that, with or without a family, we are adults with needs that have to be met.

Alone is when you realize that no one *has* to love you. Or care for you. Or be with you. Or make it possible for you to be happy. Alone is when you realize that all those things are your responsibility and always were, even when you thought you were not alone. Or when you were waiting for your life to be given some purpose. Alone is when you begin to understand that home is not a place you left behind, but the place where you find that you belong in the world.

Because we are adults, not infants, we can begin to deal with our fear of being abandoned, rejected, and deprived of love. We can discover that being lonely and being alone are not the same. Loneliness is not knowing who you are, and waiting for others to tell you. But *alone* is being aware *that* you are—and that you are a distinct part of the complicated world that surrounds you. Loneliness is waiting to be touched. Alone is reaching out toward those you love and need. And you begin by reaching out to God.

For what?

For your identity. For an appreciation of your value as a person—and that has nothing to do with how many people love you or whether you do or don't have a family. It has everything to do with the fact that you were created by Someone who wants very much to have a lasting relationship with you.

Which Comes First—Love or Identity?

You are not far from the point at which Christ stood when He was among us. Like Him, you may have to choose between searching for love or finding yourself. Being a whole person enables us to love. But being loved doesn't always enable us to become whole. It is important to understand which comes first.

It is very hard for us to love one another truly— because of what we want love to accomplish. And it cannot. Love cannot make us worthy. It cannot create what we feel is missing in us. It cannot erase what is faulty. Or mend what is broken. Or hide what we do not want to be seen. Love is not a stamp of approval, or the cavalry coming to our rescue—although we keep insisting that it must be. Love cannot do for us what we must do for ourselves.

Certainly Christ was loved. Not by everyone, and not always for what He was. And certainly He was not accurately perceived. Among those who sought Him,

He was admired and even adored for what they thought He was. Or wanted Him to be. Even the human family in which He grew up became impatient when He behaved in ways that were different from theirs. His close friends, many of whom gave up their livelihood to be with Him, felt betrayed by His death. They didn't really think He meant what He said. Surely He didn't *have* to submit to the verdict of a corrupt government? This Man who had driven out demons, who had restored sight to the blind, who had taken out His wrath on a tree that would not yield fruit out of season— surely at the last minute He would do what they all expected Him to do: seize control of the world. Poor Peter, trembling in the courtyard as an angry mob was entertained with the spectacle of a beaten Christ. Perhaps it wasn't so strange the he denied knowing the Man. Perhaps it was only at that moment that Peter began to understand who Christ was.

Since He was partly human, Christ must have known how pleasurable it felt to be loved by others, even if that love was incomplete. He must have known the warmth of being welcomed, of a space being made for Him no matter how crowded the room. He must have seen the devotion in their eyes when He spoke. He saw them pushing close to the road when He approached, stretching out their arms to touch Him. Those were the times that made up for the other moments when He was refused admission, ridiculed, argued with, cursed at. One small gesture of love can always ease the sting of rejection. And in those times of being loved, however inadequately, He must have wondered if there were not some way He could hold on to them. Did He have to give them up?

No. He had options. He could have remained in the shelter of family life. He could have been a king or a revolutionary. A theologian. An itinerant preacher. A country craftsman. If love was what He sought, then He knew any number of places where He could find it. And bask in it for as long as it lasted.

But Christ wasn't seeking love. What He sought was to make His identity known. Because love—real love—is part of our identity. Christ knew what is so difficult for all of us to realize: that if we seek love before we know who we are, then we may never find our real identity—and never find genuine love. Because we may have to become what others want us to be—and only for as long as that is what they want.

We cannot possibly be what God created and what others want us to become. They are not the same. Each of us is unique. And whenever anyone, however well intentioned, tries to alter what we truly are, they tamper with our individuality. They give us straight noses—exactly like a lot of other noses—when the bump in our nose was distinctly ours. They remove some lines and a mole here and there so that we can be beautiful in their eyes. And when we look in the mirror, we, too, may be pleased with what we see. Yet what we see is an image that conceals, not a reflection of what is. It can keep us from going on to wholeness by promising us closeness with other human beings.

Like every other person, you have some rough edges. You can't fit into any kind of a hole, round or square. You can try. You can put up with discomfort. You can make yourself over. You can promise and be promised in return. But you can't give what you don't have. And you can't withhold what you do have if someone doesn't want it.

You're stuck with yourself. And no one else is. You can't walk away from yourself. Anyone else can.

What you can do is fool yourself. And someone else as well. You can persuade yourself that it is more important to play a part than to be yourself. Especially if you don't know who you really are. The smile of approval in the eyes of another can make you give up the search for yourself. The words "I love you" can make you only too willing to be created, not by God, but by someone else. You can feel noble meeting someone else's needs and forsaking your own. You can tell yourself that being close is the same as being loved. Until, unexpectedly, one of your rough edges brushes harshly against the life you are trying to share. And the closeness is over, because it never was able to deal with conflict, with differences, with whole human beings whose lives touch, sometimes with bruising force.

Danger—Life Ahead!

Why do we do these things to each other? Why do we cling together so compulsively, yet tremble at the first sign of conflict? Why do you and I try to squeeze ourselves into each other's lives?

We call it love, but that isn't what we mean. We want shelter. We're afraid to face life alone. We don't believe we can. We want to be shielded from the world, from the way the world changes and demands new responses from us. We feel safer in the company of others. That way, we can avoid decisions, even if we don't like what is finally decided. If we have to take risks, we can share the anxiety. And if there is failure, we can blame it on someone else.

Yes, the world appears to be much safer when one is not alone.

Except that, as long as we are looking at life from behind the shelter of someone else, we cannot possibly discover our own ability to cope with it. We were created to meet life head-on, to learn from it who we are. It is this one-on-one experience of discovery that prepares us to enjoy a full and successful relationship with someone else. Because a relationship is the interaction of whole human beings—who are sometimes close, sometimes separate, not always in agreement, yet, in the long run, deeply comforting and supportive.

Don't misunderstand. The search for the self is not an act of vanity. It is not the forsaking of others and their needs. It is not the single-minded pursuit of our own interests. It is an attempt to find out what God had in mind when He created us—and then to bring those qualities into the real world.

Difficult? In one sense, yes. Because an identity is not something we can slip over our shoulders and be snug in. It is not a style of behavior. Or a set of rules that govern all of life's situations. Identity is far more elusive, yet far more simple. Our identity is our way of meeting life. It is constantly being shaped by our reaction to life, by our discovery of what we are and are not, what we can and cannot do. It is never the same from one moment to the next.

Don't be afraid of change. It can be disruptive. It makes habits obsolete, routines meaningless; it has no respect for plans and dreams. But change is life's way of reminding us that God made us flexible. If yesterday's dreams don't fit today's needs, we have the ability to dream all over again. In new ways. If we know now that life may not offer us a partnership, or that partnerships don't last forever, we can deal with those realities. We can change our dreams.

No two of us will ever meet life in the same way. You and I may have similar abilities, but we will use them differently even if we meet the same situations. We may have similar attitudes, but we will express them differently. You may have more strength than I do, but your fears may be greater. We both may enjoy a good laugh, but not for the same reasons. I may cry openly, while you bite back your tears. I may avoid the problems you take on. But I may have more patience in dealing with them once I realize that I can't get around them.

You may prefer action while I may be contemplative. Perhaps you can make decisions quickly, while I have to consider all the possibilities. You may be able to function brilliantly in a group, while I am lost in one. Do you like to work outdoors? I can spend hours at my desk.

Neither one of us is right or wrong, good or bad. We are simply the way we are. And while God can accept

34

that, very often we can't. But, then, we do not generally agree with God about who we are and what we are doing here.

The Gift We Already Have

Creation is an act of love, and the very fact that we are alive means that we are loved. Not necessarily by the others in our life. But certainly by God.

The elements that go into something that is created are not always remarkable. Colors, words, sounds, thoughts, lines, voices, energy, cells, light, weight—and more than we could ever list. But it is love—the creator's love—that brings them all together into something that makes sense in the world, into something that answers a need in the world. And the creator's love is there before the creation takes shape. It sees what can be, and that is what the creator loves. That understanding of how the creation fits into the world is the creation's identity, the key to what the creation is and always will be. The creation *is* the creator's love—made visible, audible, touchable.

Each one of us is the visible, audible, touchable form of God's love for the world. We are His creation, and only He really knows what went into the making of us. Only He knows how valuable we are and how much the world needs each one of us. No one else will ever see in us what He sees. No one else will ever know our whole selves so intimately.

The creation itself is the creator's reward. Nothing more is asked. But along with pleasure at what is created, the creator must also experience a certain amount of pain when no one else can fully appreciate what has been accomplished. Some will even call it shabby, false, foolish. Some will try to make it over as they want it to be. Some will discard it as worthless. The creation may be marred by abuse, disregard, negligence, and exaggeration. Nevertheless, the creator knows its worth. His love is still part of it.

Some of our best qualities as human beings go unappreciated in this world. If we are patient, we may be called stubborn or not too bright. If we have trust, we may be seen as foolish. If we call a spade a spade, then we're just no fun. If we stand up to giants, we're show-offs. Honesty is fine, we're told, but not all the time; some people consider it disloyal. Generosity is out of style; it's said to encourage weakness.

We are under a great deal of pressure to change what we are for what the world would rather have us be. And very often we do. We follow the trends. We become street-smart. We cut corners, tell only part of the truth, betray confidences, make promises we can't keep, avoid confrontations—especially when we know there's a chance we might get hurt. We give unto Caesar, but not unto anyone else. We divide problems into categories: ours and theirs. And then we wonder why life doesn't seem to have any meaning.

Well, it does. And so do we. What we were, and what we can become, is still a part of us. But perhaps a part that only God can see.

This original concept, this love of God for what we are, is the self in each of us. It is always there, no matter what happens to us, no matter how many different images we try to assume, no matter how much damage is done to us. We sense it, but we can't describe it because we haven't dared to allow it to shape our lives—to become visible. We have tried, instead, to find in other people the love that God has already given to us and will never take back. And we haven't succeeded. Because instead of looking for love, we have to look for ourselves. *That* is where the love is.

Not to be kept for our own use. Not to shelter us from life. We need God's love to guide is into an understanding of ourselves—not as winners or losers, but as fully developed human beings who are good at some things and not at others. Who have surprising strengths and many weaknesses. Who can be hurt as deeply through someone else's pain as from our own. Who can trust again even after being betrayed. Who can survive disappointment. Who can give when there is very little. Who can listen—and hear—when something can't be put into words. Who are as open to joy as to sorrow. Who can be part of the lives of others without giving up our own.

This is who we are. This is what we are doing here.

Right now, whether you're ready or not, you have a choice to make. Being alone can be depressing, terrifying, isolating. Or it can be rewarding, worth all the struggles, the irritations, the fear, confusion, pain, and exploration that you are going to experience. It is neither the best nor the worst time of your life, but rather a time of challenge. And God is going to do the challenging—if you will allow Him. He's going to insist that you go on to become the person He created a long time ago. Not all by yourself, but with His help. Instead of secluding you from life, He's going to push you right into the middle of it—and go with you.

First of all, He's going to teach you how to take care of yourself. Then He's going to prove to you that your life is far from over.

3

YES—SOMEONE IS THERE

I USED TO ENJOY being alone when I was young. Some of my happiest moments were spent curled up on the corner of my bed next to the window, with a drowsy dog beside me and a lined yellow pad on my knees. I loved to put my thoughts on paper.

They were comfortable times, with no one else around. But, as I say, I was a child then. And I was part of a family. Being alone was a pleasurable little island where I could spend time as I pleased. I could also end it whenever I chose. It was not a way of life, and I never expected that it would be.

I was mistaken about that, as many of us are. Years later I did find myself alone, and it was not an island. Aloneness was an alien world that I had no choice but to enter, and my early experiences there made me promise myself that I would escape.

On the afternoon of the first day I was truly alone, I had to make a simple decision that suddenly became very difficult for me: What was I going to have for dinner? And how much food should I cook for one? On which side of the table did I want to sit? Ridiculous questions, you may think. And the strange part of it is that I couldn't remember ever considering them before. I just used to *do* things; choice wasn't important or even necessary. And I found it irritating to be faced with choices and decisions every time I turned around. For instance, when I moved into a smaller house and there was painting to be done, the salesclerk in the paint store asked me what colors I wanted, and I couldn't answer right away. I didn't know because I had never asked myself what colors I liked. I always chose colors I knew other people liked because my pleasure was in pleasing. When it was time to please myself, I didn't know how.

Perhaps because I didn't feel I was worth pleasing. I even felt uncomfortable making the attempt because I wasn't accustomed to giving my time, my attention, and my concern to myself.

I didn't understand until much later that decisions are a necessary part of maturity. They are more than irritating; they are awesome reminders that no one else can live our lives for us. That unless we decide exactly what we are going to do this minute and the next, nothing will get done. And as much as we may wish for someone to take us by the hand and lead us one step forward, it won't happen. We will not move ahead unless our own feet take us there, one step at a time.

But—how does a woman learn to make decisions? In a hurry?

She doesn't. She already knows how.

I used to think a decision was a momentous solution to a major problem. Sometimes it is. But most of the time our problems are small and our decisions go unnoticed, even by ourselves. I had forgotten how many times I had made decisions about little things: How to buy what my family needed with the amount of money available; what kind of food to eat, how to prepare it; how to dress for the day; how to get to the train when the car wasn't available; how to get those books back to the library; how to remember to change my dentist appointment, to call a friend who was starting a new job, to get some stamps and go to the bank; how to find a typist for the book I was writing—and how to find more time to work on it.

I left the bigger decisions to someone else: Whether to get a new furnace, how much of our money we could afford to invest—and in what; where to go on vacation; whether to get a new car or make do with the old one; how to deal with a promotion that meant moving to another part of the country. I didn't feel qualified to handle the big decisions; I told myself that I lacked experience. But the truth was that I lacked the willingness to take responsibility for my life. Because making a decision is another way of taking a certain direction in life. We open a door and go through it. Granted, there is some risk involved—because we can't always turn around and go back the way we came. That was the part that scared me.

What do you do if you can't go back?

You find another way to go on. It's not the same as running out of one food and substituting another—but it's not that different, either. Not as long as you realize that you are the one who has to take that step—and that if you can't take it the first time, you keep trying until you do. The result is called *competence*—not a particularly glorious term, but a satisfying sense of being at home in the world.

I remember a day not very long after I was alone when I had to face a number of problems, all but one of them small. I had to go out of town on business, so I had to board my cat and dog. The kennel, a good one, is quite far from my home. And I didn't like leaving my pets because I needed their companionship. On the way back from the kennel, I was scheduled for a physical examination required for insurance purposes. In the afternoon I had to see my lawyer, pick up my coat from the cleaner—and I had promised a friend I would look over a speech she had written. Oh, yes, I had to pack.

When I awoke that morning, I was already exhausted from wondering how I would fit so many things into one day. But out of habit I began making breakfast, just as I always did. It never occurred to me that that simple act involved a lot of decisions—until I was driving away from my house with my cat and dog in my car. I looked in the mirror and say my dog's eyes. They were calm. She trusted me. My cat, in his carrying case on the seat beside me, was resigned, as he always is when we go to the kennel. And I realized that I was a grown-up woman taking care of herself and her family. Nothing fancy. No big deal. Just competent. I could handle it. I would feel the pressure, but so does everyone else who has a lot to do. To this day, competence is one of the most delicious sensations I have ever known.

Being on your own can make you feel useless. Does

it matter what time you get up in the morning—as long as you get to work on time? If you leave your bed unmade or never run a dustcloth over your furniture, who will notice? Why dirty a plate when you can throw a sandwich together and eat it standing at the sink? Maybe you don't own a decent chair or your mattress looks like a canoe, but there's just you, so what difference does it make?

It is much easier to be of use to others instead of being ourselves in a relationship with others. It is much easier to please someone else instead of ourselves, to give someone else the responsibility for making us happy. Or the blame for our misery. It is why so many of us resist becoming spiritually and emotionally adult. And why we have not taken up the challenge of a mature relationship with God—or anyone else. We don't know *how* to be responsible for ourselves. We never thought we would have to be, so we never had a reason to explore our strengths. It's not so different from the way we used to think of our athletic abilities. How can we use muscles we don't know we have?

Single men have had an easier time of it. They were never considered to be alone. While none of us, man or woman, take eagerly to a solitary way of life, men are allowed by others a certain amount of it without penalty. Men are accepted as the forgers-ahead, the finders of paths—roles one usually must undertake alone. And it is assumed that somewhere a family waits for them or that they will be starting one. Men have always been expected to build a life for themselves; women have not—for the simple reason that, "Why should they? Someone else will do it for them."

Single women may resent the fact that single men are more often invited to dinner at the homes of married friends. We may resent the accolades men are given for ordinary achievements in the kitchen. We may loathe the reality that it is not a good idea to list our first name in the telephone directory—it's safer to use initials and thereby be mistaken for a man. We may not like having to prove that we can think clearly, logically, on any day of the month. But we may not have considered another important reality: that men are burdened with a reputation they don't deserve. In some of their recent writings, and more often in their conversations, men are beginning to reveal that they are not naturally brave, resourceful, rational, and always at ease in society. They are beginning to admit that they tremble every bit as much as women do, faced with similar situations, yet they are not generally allowed the opportunity to reveal their insecurities. Nor are they permitted the freedom to decide whether they will face a crisis or run for cover. Their traditional assignment is to stand and fight to the last—because they are supposed to be able to perform such feats with a facility that women do not possess.

So it has been said. But we—both men and women—are learning that what has been said is not the same as what is.

Someday we may realize that the very men we women depended upon to lead us into the presence of God have never actually been there. They are only assumed to have been, and we can imagine how difficult it must be for any man who feels he does not know God to admit it. We might even be the first ones to accuse him of betrayal when he is only being honest. Unless we too break free of the roles history has imposed upon men, we may not be aware that many of them hunger for the same spiritual relationship that we ourselves are beginning to seek.

We could spend the rest of our lives, like infants, in protest against everyone who failed to prepare us for the real world. Except that they did prepare us for the only world they knew: theirs. And ours is different. We could bemoan the loss of those we depended upon to take care of us. Except that we may have depended a little too much for their good and ours. Again, it's the way people used to live, and they don't anymore. That is what happens when we insist on learning about life from one another instead of learning about life from God Himself.

The Need to Grow

It was a shock for me to discover that being alone later in life was not the same as being alone as a little girl. I tried curling up with a pad on my knees and a drowsy dog next to me, but I couldn't avoid the knowledge that these were not a few precious moments that I could bring to an end at any time. I had no idea when my aloneness was going to end, or how. My yellow pad, like my life, was blank. I couldn't think of a word to write.

Nor was I at ease in the presence of God. I was self-conscious because I felt Him frowning at me. He had always seemed to smile when I was a child. He seemed so close that I could share my thoughts with Him as spontaneously as I scribbled them on paper. I even wrote some poems about Him; I'm glad I didn't save them because they were quite awful, even for a child to write. But they did demonstrate that I felt accepted by God. I had no difficulty thinking of Him as my Father; it made me feel secure.

But I was no longer a child, and behaving like one was out of place. I had some adult problems to solve, and I had the distinct impression that God was urging me to grow up—fast.

We had it out, God and I, one evening when I was trying to fasten four legs onto a circular tabletop I needed for my new dining room. I'm clumsy with tools and I was fighting reality with a passion, furious at my helplessness. Under my breath I was blaming God for my situation and finally I blamed Him out loud, tears and all. In some peculiar way I think I expected Him to put the table together for me. But of course He didn't. The table was still there, in pieces, when my tantrum had run its course. But I felt His presence—and there it was again, the conviction that He was frowning at me. I couldn't blame Him. Much more serious problems were ahead of me. How was I going to handle them?

Nevertheless I looked for an easy way out. I called a carpenter who had done some work for me. Could he put the legs on my table? Well, he could, he said, but he wouldn't feel right about charging me for something I could easily do myself. "Here's what you do," he said. "Get an awl. . . ." Obviously God wasn't letting me off the hook. He was not going to put my table *or* my life together. He meant for me to do both.

Never mind what an awl is, I got one and it did what I hadn't been able to do, and later that evening I had a dining-room table with legs on it. I was quite proud of myself. And I did not feel the least bit like a child when I said, "It's a little wobbly, Lord, but I think it'll hold up." The statement was true of me as well.

That was several years ago, and since that time I have had to make many more decisions, most of them far more complex than what to cook for dinner or how to put legs on a table. But always there was that underlying ultimatum: *You* are the one who has to decide. *You* are the one who is responsible for you.

I learned that from God. In fact, I think I grew up in His presence and at His insistence. It was the only way we could relate to each other.

A New Friend

I'm not saying that God solved all my problems or that He enabled me to endure what couldn't be solved. But He was there when no one else was. He was incredibly patient with my fumbling attempts to find out what I could do about the rest of my life. He did come to my rescue several times, and He let me lean on Him when I had to stop for breath. He allowed me to discover my strengths and weaknesses so that I could make better or less use of them. He often taught me something valuable through my mistakes. And He let me discover that I am not so easily knocked down, and that I can usually get up again. My common sense and judgment needed a great deal of exercise, and He gave me the grace to forgive myself when I used them carelessly. He also gave me the courage to be as open with others as I have learned to be with Him.

He somehow prevented disappointment from getting the better of me, especially when disappointment followed disappointment. That was particularly important because I used to think that disappointment meant I was going in the wrong direction. I thought that if I did the right thing, in the right manner, I would automatically find fulfillment. It was my childish way of expecting God to put Stop and Go signs in my path: disappointment meant Stop and fulfillment meant Go. I know now that both disappointment and fulfillment are natural consequences of life; so are pleasure and pain. I know, too, that God has given me the resourcefulness to deal with both the ups and the downs, no matter how many times they repeat themselves.

Through all of these experiences I was finding out not only who God is, but who I am. Perhaps I needed to know one before I could understand the other. I know now, for instance, that God understands me, a woman, every bit as well as He seems to understand the men I have known. He has helped me to understand that my feelings are not to be put aside. They are not playthings; they have value in the world. My sensitivity, far from being a handicap in practical areas, is another way of gathering information about what is going on in the lives and minds and hearts of others. He also understands what it means to be without a person you love. He parted with His Son, remember? He knows the frustration of waiting for recognition; we taught Him that, too. He knows everything there is to know about solitude, its blessings and its agonies.

He knows me particularly well, as well as He knows you. He has allowed my experiences to show me that I am more capable than I thought, yet far more vulnerable in ways I didn't expect. I am beginning to realize that my patience has its limits, and if I don't pay attention to them, I may become depressed. I can wait for the good things in life, but, oh, how I do enjoy them! I can do without—as long as I can hope. I love very hard, I trust a little too quickly, but I have stopped being afraid to love and to be hurt. I know now that the sharpest pain can end, the deepest wound can heal.

I am not a lonely person. I have no reason to be. My life is well populated with good relationships, and I treasure them. I think it all begin when I realized that God is more than Parent. He is Friend. And through His friendship for me I have learned how to be a friend to myself, and a better friend to others than I have ever been.

Then why didn't I seek this friendship earlier in my life? And, especially, earlier in my aloneness?

Good question. But the answer will not be the same for all of us. I had to deal with my lingering guilt over a broken marriage. Mary, a widowed friend, didn't want to admit how much she blamed God for the death of her husband. And Allison, whom I've mentioned before, felt that God couldn't possibly understand her because she wasn't following His game plan.

Plausible reasons, all of them. They are, nevertheless, excuses.

The real reason why we keep our distance from God is that we expect Him to rescue us from our circumstances. And we are disappointed when He doesn't. He doesn't make the rain go away. He doesn't promise us, just as we are falling asleep, that everything is going to be fine in the morning. He isn't at all what we expect Him to be. And that is the part of God that makes it difficult for us to have a relationship with Him. He will not be manipulated. He will not do for us what we can do for ourselves.

Forgetting How to Be Helpless

When we were children, we were too small to do anything about our circumstances. We needed to be lifted out of difficulty by someone bigger, stronger. We needed someone to open doors that stuck, someone to be there when we came home, a cool hand on a fevered brow, sympathy for a bruised knee, a hug for a good report card, praise for a task completed, and a special treat for a special accomplishment. Everything we did was noticed; we were either good or bad, but we weren't ignored.

Such things are hard to give up.

Actually we don't have to. God will not abandon us

as adults. He will continue to give us the care and protection that a child needs—but only at great cost to Him and to us. Our current needs are different, often greater, than those of a child. But as long as we deny them, we deny God the opportunity to do something about them. As caring a Father as God is, He is also a loyal, supportive Friend, a delightful Companion, a compassionate Teacher, and a fierce Ally who will lay down His life for us—again—if necessary. Yet we can know Him only as a Father unless we have the courage to become more than children. And it is through the experience of finding more of God that we find more of ourselves. As we begin to see ourself through God's eyes, we will find a person worthy of devotion and encouragement, a person whose presence brings joy, a willing learner, and someone so beloved as to make sacrifice possible. This is the person each of us can become.

Can We?

To this day I shudder whenever it is time for me to do something about my life. I know I can avoid it. I can wait and hope that the problem will go away. Or that someone else will solve it for me. That is the kind of person I once was. But I'm not the same anymore. I know that I was not created to stand still. God has also given me the ability to move. And to move *things*.

I used to think that women were passive. I saw nothing wrong with that; we seemed to balance men and their inclination toward action. We could think of comforting words for stressful situations. From scarce resources we could put together an environment that welcomed, that closed the door securely upon the world's anxieties. We could renew spent energy, inspire hope, applaud emerging ideas. We had the patience to be bombarded by growing young minds, the insight to understand and respond to the way other people felt.

We fit in so well. Wasn't that enough?

No. Because it didn't use all that we are.

None of us, neither men nor women, are meant to fit into someone else's life. We are meant to have lives of our own. Lives that we can share with others—without giving up any part of them.

I also used to think that men found it easy to act. To do. To change not only their lives but the face of the world. But I was wrong.

Men are beginning to acknowledge that they find it just as difficult to act as women do. They, too, would rather be passive persons because they are not confident of their ability to take on the world. They are like modern-day disciples, begging Christ not to leave them because there is so much He can do for them. And Christ, loving them as only God can love, has tried to make them understand that only on their own can they discover how able they are. But it often isn't enough for them to be assured that Christ will be with them spiritually. They want *Him*, right here, where He can protect them. They don't like what He sees in them. They don't want to be courageous. Or dedicated. They don't want to go beyond their own neighborhoods. They don't want to take a stand. Or confront evil. Or walk forth on a lonely road, not knowing where they will eat or sleep or find a friend. They don't want to suffer or sacrifice—or any of the other things that men are supposed to do so naturally.

Neither of us, men nor women, are created only to move or only to stand still. There is the potential for both in each of us, but we feel awkward using abilities that we have long associated exclusively with the other.

Someone to Count On

Recently I had the unusual experience of sharing with my stepfather what I have learned about being alone. It began after my mother died and my stepfather was faced with being alone after fifty years of marriage. For the last six years of my mother's life, while she was an invalid, my stepfather was her nurse and companion. He learned to cook. He made their home shine the way my mother once did, and his good humor and pleasant conversation prevented my mother from ever feeling that she was a burden. He learned to do so many things that men are not required to do. And he did them well.

During those six years, my stepfather left his house only for an hour at a time. My mother, of course, could not travel at all. And since we lived some distance from each other, we saw each other only when I visited them. They both realized that I had begun to live alone, but I don't think they could identify with my way of life because they had each other. Besides, they were facing a much more serious situation than mine. I said very little about myself other than that I was fine. If I was not the same as I used to be, I covered it up. Consequently, when my stepfather was able to visit me in my own home again, we were like two friends who hadn't seen each other in a long time. We weren't the same people anymore.

Each of us had grown more in the last few years than in all the many years since I had lived at home with my parents.

My stepfather noticed that when he came to visit me after my mother's death. "You're very independent," he said. Not in a critical tone. He was pleased. "You're a good driver," he told me—and I knew he didn't think many people were. For the first time in our years together, he asked me questions about my work—not the writing part of it but the business part. Then he told me stories about his days as a salesman and the accounts he opened that were still doing well. Wonderful stories that I had never heard before. He brought me coupons for some of the items I buy in the supermarket; I never had the patience to cut them out, but he convinced me that they could save me a lot of money. I was planning to move out into the country. And he understood that. He didn't think I would be isolated. "You can handle it," he said. "Space is good for you."

I taught him how to shop for one person. How to ask for a better table in a restaurant. What to keep on hand for friends who stopped in. I convinced him to buy a new car because even though his old one had very few miles on it, it had seen better days.

Our favorite times, whenever he visits, are the moments when I am preparing a meal and he is sitting at the kitchen table. That's when we talk about sports, possibly because I have learned a lot about sports since I was a young girl living at home, and my stepfather was always a sports fan. We don't always root for the same teams, but we respect each other's opinions.

I understand why my stepfather wants to stay where he is rather than move closer to my home. He is holding on to the memory of my mother. Holding on, also, to people who know him by name. Yet he understands why I want to break new ground.

We have learned something about each other in these later years. We know that within each of us the yearning to enjoy life is pitted against the ability to meet life's demands. Neither of us is passive or active: Each of us is both. This realization has brought us closer together. My stepfather's ability to act gave me the protection I needed when I was growing up and couldn't look out for myself. Now I think he finds comfort in the knowledge that I can look after him in his later years. He doesn't articulate it in the way that many younger men do, but he may be relieved to realize that he doesn't have to go on being the one who solves problems and makes decisions. There is more to him than that.

Perhaps that is what maturity really is—an acknowledgment that although we would like to enjoy serenity for the rest of our lives, we are willing to do what must be done to take our place in the world.

More Than Give-and-Take

My stepfather and I do more than look after each other. We have a relationship. And the difference is important. I can look after you without knowing anything about you except what you need. And you can receive what I have to give without knowing my identity. The give-and-take is strictly between us—and for our own benefit. But a relationship involves more than you and me; it includes what we are trying to accomplish. So if you and I are going to have a relationship, if we are going to combine what we are in order to accomplish something, then we have to make ourselves known to each other. We have to be aware of what is going into our joint effort. Not that each of us must match what the other has to give. Not that you must contribute what I don't have. But that each of us gives our whole selves—the good, the bad, and all the in-between—to our common cause. And that cause can be anything from a desire to help each other grow into whole human beings, to the raising of a child and the making of a home, to a job that needs to be done, or the improvement of something that is not right in the world. Being together simply because we like each other, or because we feel more secure in each other's company, is not a relationship. It is closeness—and even two strangers can be close. I can be close to you and not be interested in anything about you other than the fact that I feel better when you are near me. I may not even want to know all there is to know about you—because I may not like all that I discover. And I may not want to deal with what I do not like.

A relationship is a challenge; closeness is not. In a real relationship we confront all that each of us is—what we like and don't like. We encourage each other to become our whole selves. On a human level, a relationship is a reflection of God's love for each of us. What we like about each other is easy to accept; what we don't like we must negotiate. Not change. Not withhold. But admit, perhaps grow impatient with, put into perspective, and even find of some value. In a relationship we have to know what abilities are available in each of us, so that we can count on them when we run into obstacles. We have to know what our weaknesses are, so that we can compensate for them. We are not asking for perfection in each other. But we are asking for the courage to be honest.

It takes a great deal of courage—and honesty—to admit that we are afraid of maturity. We see it as the end of the care we expected as children, the demolition of all our shelters, the exposure of our unprotected selves to the harshness of a callous world. And in many ways it is all of that. But maturity is also the end of the myth that if we remain as children we will be safe. We won't. We weren't—even when we were children. If we really try, any one of us can remember times of fear when we were children. So much of life was bigger than we were, and threatening. But, being children, we sensed that it was not our place to ward off danger.

Adults could, but we couldn't—or so it appeared. And many of us assumed that the adults we trusted to look after us were somehow endowed—almost magically—with strength and competence.

We still make that same assumption about other people. Somehow they seem to be able to handle adult life while we can't. They seem to have the judgment, the stamina, and the unshakability that we seem to lack. Can't we just let them be mature while we remain children? Can't each of us just do what comes naturally to us?

Yes—as long as we understand what is "natural."

Growth is a natural part of life. It is a continuously replenished, constantly changing, always available source of the energy we need to live in this world. It equips us, if we choose to use it, to move from childhood into maturity, from childlike dependency on God to companionship with Him. From "Help me!" to "Enable me."

There is nothing magical about growth. Neither is it an automatic process. The adults we knew as children—and those we know today—have not had an easy time of it. The world is big and threatening to them, too. They are uncertain about their ability to survive in it. The wrenches of life come upon them as suddenly as they do to us, disrupting the serenity they so desire. Keeping a low profile hasn't protected them anymore than it has us. Life *will* get at us. And because God knows that far better than we do, He has created us with the potential to meet such times. We don't look forward to them, and most of us, if we could, would bypass maturity and all its responsibilities. But we can't—and God knows that, too.

Christ was not at His most popular when He spoke to us about discovering our strengths. We still tend to blame Him for allowing anything unpleasant to happen to us. *Let us lie here where we have fallen*, we tell Him. *Someone will come along and pick us up.* And of course no one does. No one can—except ourselves, with the help of God reaching out to us. No, God has not abandoned us. He waits for us to take His hand. He will wait forever. But if He must wait that long, and if we don't reach out, we will never experience the end of our fear of growing up. We will never discover how well equipped we are to live in this world.

One of the most courageous and honest people I know is a woman whose husband saw more in her than she saw in herself. Today Marcia is a devoted friend who can visit a sickroom even when her arm is in a sling after a bad fall on the ice. She is a physician who is concerned about the lives of her patients. She is a mother who understands her handicapped daughter's determination to be independent—and encourages her. She was not always able to give that much.

Quite some years ago, Marcia was a wife, a mother, and a grade-school teacher. She enjoyed her life, although she thought it was a little too busy. She was always promising herself that she would take some time off and just do nothing. Then her husband suddenly became ill, and the prognosis was more than Marcia could handle. Gil wasn't going to recover. "I was desperate, I was furious, I was absolutely heartbroken," she says. "Gil was too young to die! I needed him. So did our daughter. And I loved him so much."

Gil didn't have much time, so he couldn't wait for Marcia to realize what was going to happen—not only that he was going to die but that she would have to provide for their family by herself.

Because Gil was so young—in his mid-thirties—he hadn't had time to provide long-term financial security for his wife and daughter. He knew that Marcia would need more than a teacher's salary, and he also remembered that Marcia had once wanted to become a doctor. Well, he told her, now was the time for it. She could go back to school, become what she always wanted to be, and earn a better living for herself and their daughter. There would be enough insurance money to pay the bills until she finished school—if she was careful. Gil's mother would move in to keep house and look after their daughter.

Marcia couldn't believe what she was hearing. How could she think about years of demanding training when her whole world was coming apart? "You have to," Gil told her. "*You have to.*"

When I met Marcia, she was a doctor specializing in geriatrics, a new field at the time. And there are people I know who remember her during her years in medical school—the long hours with little sleep, the difficult classes, the exams that showed no mercy, the solemn atmosphere of hospital wards and the struggle to pull life from the hands of death. Marcia was older than the other students, but somehow she found the energy to keep up with them. She had excellent grades. She cared about the patients. And she was always good for a laugh at the right moment.

"I didn't know I could do it," she told me. "But Gil did. He knew me so well, he could see things I didn't know were there. I think the most loving words he ever said to me were: *You have to.* He wasn't talking to the woman I thought I was—he was talking to the *real* me."

Who Will Go with You?

The search for the self is not a short journey. The distance from who you are to what you can be is vast. It can't be traveled quickly; it will take your lifetime.

Much of the journey is over rough ground in unfamiliar places. You won't always be welcome. The accommodations, when available, may be as simple as a smile or as rare as the look of understanding in the eyes of another person.

You will feel inept in the beginning. You won't always know what to do next. Your reactions will occasionally surprise you, because you didn't know you had such feelings. Such determination. Such an ability to experience what is going on in someone else's life. In time, though, you will feel more at home in the world—and in yourself.

You will see things in the world that you didn't see before. You'll find more beauty than you expected, but also more waste when that beauty has been marred. You will not like a lot of the things you see, and you will want to help change them. And you will know, from having traveled a small part of your journey, that you *can* make a difference. That you can put together not only a life for yourself, but perhaps a few broken pieces of the world as well.

You? All by yourself? You can do all that?

Not quite.

From the moment we take a step toward our maturity, we are in the company of God. Not as infants in His arms, but as travelers together on a road to discovery. To responsibility. To usefulness. To the softness of serenity—and the harshness of action. To tears of frustration—and the long, slow exhale of achievement. To turning back. And turning around again. To finding other ways.

To completing—with His help—what God started a long time ago. He can go as far, and give as much, as you need. Take what He offers. Ask for more. Use it. Act on it. Do something with it.

You can.

4

THE PERSON KNOWN

AS YOU

"IT'S A GOOD THING you don't have children. You've got enough to worry about," one of my friends said when she learned I was alone.

Another friend said, "I wish you had children. They'd be such a comfort."

I did have an elderly dog and a youngish cat, and I cared for them deeply. "You're so tied down," one friend said.

"They're such good company for you," said another.

All of which indicates how important it is to know what *you* want in your life. I was fifty years old before I came upon that valuable little lesson. Before that, my life was filled with my attempts to meet a lot of other people's expectations. I wasn't unhappy. Winning approval of those you love can be a beautiful experience. Pleasing those you care about gives you a very strong sense of belonging. But when you suddenly find yourself alone, cut off from those other expectations, you begin to wonder who on earth you are. Worse than that, you begin to wonder why on earth you're here, because there doesn't seem to be any reason for your existence. And many people try to end that existence because they don't have a reason of their own for going on. Others try to squeeze themselves into a role so that at least they can become someone recognizable, even if only as a type.

Being alone does not label us. It does not proclaim that we were once lovable and now we are not. It does not insist that, because caring got us nowhere, we must now stop caring. Becoming responsible for ourselves does not mean that we are no longer responsible for others. Even for others who do not love us.

There is nothing either/or about being alone, because it is not a role. It is not a reduced way of life. It is a possibility for us to participate in a highly creative endeavor: the discovery of our whole selves. It is a time of preparation for a full life—but by that I do not mean a life filled with all that is good and glorious and delightful. With a full life, we get some of everything: the surprises and the endless repetitions, the hurts and the pleasures, the leaning and being leaned on, truth and falsehood, generosity and deprivation, none of it evenly distributed. And through our openness to these experiences we gradually make our own acquaintance. Not by handling life well or badly, but by meeting it, reacting to it, being wrong and sometimes being right, and sometimes being right because we have already been wrong and can now recognize the difference between the two. We have this ability to meet life. We got it from God, but we are the ones who have to make use of it. Like anything creative, it is something one has to do alone. Only the results of our creative endeavor can be shared.

Is It Safe Here?

Understandably, roles are hard to resist. They are so available, like clothing bought off the rack. So much is specified that there is little room for error. And it may be our fear of making mistakes that causes us to assume behavior and qualities that do not really express who we are. We wear what is in style even though we can see that it doesn't compliment us. Yet we can always convince ourselves that we're acceptable because we look just like everyone else.

Acceptable? Is that really so important?

Yes. Because it is safe. And a role is a refuge—from being hurt.

A young woman I now count as a friend is someone I didn't like at all when we first met. She is attractive, intelligent, and good company. Exciting ideas make her conversation sparkle, and she can put you at ease with a gutsy laugh that insists you join in. But she is also brash, superficial, and a bit of a conniver; the laugh can end as suddenly as it begins when things don't go her way. She is a buyer for a large department store and she is very proud of hiring people—mostly single-parent women who "sure can use a job." But the truth is that she hires people who have good reason to fear losing a job, and they are easily intimidated.

"Please, don't ask me to dinner if Barbara's going to be there," I pleaded with the friend who had introduced us. And my friend, who is far more perceptive than I am, kept bringing us together.

Finally I began to understand why.

Barbara is a phony. Underneath the hard surface of an accomplished businesswoman, she is a sensitive human being. But she's also scared—because she sees too many things in this world that truly are frightening: men in late middle age (her father was one of them), laid off by a company that had promised them lifelong security, men too young for a pension and too old to start over again; women, like her mother, fighting off depression because they don't feel they have a purpose in life. Some of Barbara's friends got married, but the marriages didn't last. Some have children and wonder what to do with them. Love? Well, it's like politics—or, better yet, a beguiling slogan: Promise them anything . . . Barbara doesn't feel she can trust anyone or anything. Except herself. So she tries not to let her feelings show.

God? She hadn't thought about Him, not since she stopped going to church a long time ago. Maybe she ought to start going again . . .

If you'll excuse the change in gender and in time, Barbara is the contemporary Rich Young Ruler toying with the idea that maybe she's missed something in life. And, like her gentlemanly forerunner, she would find Christ's terms unpalatable. He would ask her to give up her role, her refuge, her self-protection. He would urge her to risk seeking her whole sensitive self. Even if she got hurt.

I used to wonder why Christ thought it was so important for a nice young man to impoverish himself. After all, what is so wrong with having money? Or power? Or even—a refuge? I did not find that poverty was a blessing in the lives of those afflicted with it. Nor did I find wealth to be an inevitable corruption. Now it occurs to me that Christ was drawing a line— not between material possessions and the lack of them, but between reality and self-deception. He was insisting that we stop hiding—behind roles, behind false security, behind anything that offers us protection from real life. He wants us exposed, because it is in meeting life that we find ourselves.

Every now and then I catch a glimpse of the real Barbara, and it is this person who is my friend. She does care about the people who work for her. She listens to their outpourings; she cries more easily for them than for herself. But she continues to rule them with an iron hand. She wouldn't dare try to build up their self-confidence because, as she puts it, "Next thing you know, they'll be after my job!" She would like to have a family, but she doesn't have time to look after anyone else. Looking out for herself is a full-time job—because she's so afraid that no one else will. "I've got to make it big, and fast, before they dump me," she says. And she believes it.

Why shouldn't she? As Barbara sees it, life is a dangerous place to be. And she believes that the only way she can protect herself is to cover up her compassion, her sensitivity, and her ability to love. She doesn't realize how much she is hurting herself by denying herself access to her finest qualities. Something is missing from Barbara's life, all right: the best part of herself.

If you were to tell Barbara that the safest thing she

can do is to become her whole self, if you were to insist that the only way she can do that is to give up her role, to come out from her refuge and enter into a full life, she would probably shake her head sadly. No doubt she would turn away, deeply concerned for your well-being but unable to relate to you by letting you know how much she cares.

It Takes Courage to Be

Self-discovery is so chancy. So full of the unexpected, the unevaluated, the unrated. It can be risky because we can't be sure we'll be acceptable—to ourselves or to others. We can't process a situation or a person; we have to react with our feelings, our willingness to understand, our experience or lack of it. We will make mistakes. We will not always be acceptable. There will be times when we will play hard ball, when we allow the flint to show in our eyes. But that does not have to make *us* hard or flinty. It requires, rather, that we be willing to use these qualities—which God gave to us along with our softer ones—when the occasion calls for them. There will be other times when we may be incredibly patient in the face of hostility because we know that we will not allow ourselves to be abused.

Hard ball is very difficult for women to play. Not that we can't. We play very well. But we would rather not play at all. Because hard ball means abandoning the passive behavior we have practiced for generations. It means demanding what we want and have earned rather than waiting for someone to give it to us—or to deny us. It means taking action, looking out for ourselves, confronting, negotiating, calling attention to our needs, and at times, pitting our strength against that of an opponent. Historically—and possibly not fairly—we left such things to men. Now, however, we often find ourselves in opposition to men because we want some of the same things men want. And not enough time has passed for men to learn how to deal with self-sufficient women.

"When men said I was pushy and aggressive, it used to bother me," a teacher friend of mine said. "I'd back down. I felt unfeminine. I'd stop asking for a better schedule of classes—I'd take whatever I was given. I ended up teaching at 8 o'clock in the morning and at 8 o'clock at night, with nothing in between. I didn't know a single man with a schedule like that. Finally I realized that if I had to be pushy and aggressive to get what was reasonable, well, then, that was part of being a woman, too."

My friend now has a realistic schedule. And she's going after a promotion. "This time I can put up with the remarks," she says goodnaturedly. "They don't distract me and make me wonder if I'm doing the right thing. I know I am. So does the opposition."

Too many of us accept the manners we have learned and the behavior we practice as ourselves. They are not. Courtesy is kindness and thoughtfulness, a concern for the sensitivities of others. But manners are conveniences; it takes less time and effort to respond to one another the way we're "supposed to" rather than the way we really feel.

Reaction is an honest response to life. But behavior may be an avoidance of it. Consequently, by being ourselves and reacting to life, we will sometimes be considered unmannerly, even badly behaved. Very much as Christ was—when He overturned the moneychangers' tables instead of registering a complaint with the Temple management; when He touched the sick and diseased instead of throwing them a coin from a safe distance; when He stooped to wash the feet of His friends instead of summoning a servant; when He interrupted, brushed people aside, spoke impatiently, even angrily, to those He loved.

In a full life, we are not out to win approval or to win the game—but to negotiate relationships between whole persons. Going from here to there is not what counts; *growing* from here to there is.

How Can You Tell If It's You?

Considering the risks involved in seeking our identity, how can we know that what we find is our genuine self?

By the feedback. By the presence or absence of anxiety.

When you are trying to live up to an image, there is a lot of noise inside of you. For everything you do, every move you make, you can hear what you expect other people to say: *I wouldn't if I were you . . . Aren't you afraid? Oh—be careful . . . That's nice—but . . . I'd rather you . . . Do you really think you can? . . . Maybe you ought to wait . . .*

When we begin to act upon what we feel about life, there is quiet within. So that we can hear what God has been trying to say to us all along: that He believes in us, that He created us to survive in the world, that He will go with us.

You will have concerns. You will meet stress, you will be faced with difficult problems and you won't always have the answers. But you will not feel as if the world is going to end. You will not be consumed with anxiety about what someone will think of you, or do to you, or say about you. You will consider, instead, what *you* can *do*—about *your* life.

There is such a thing as pleasing yourself. That doesn't mean you can't also please someone else, but it does mean that you begin to get a sense of your own identity. What is it about you that makes you what you are? That makes you feel the way you feel? How does this knowledge influence the choices you make about the kind of life you will have? It's unfortunate if you have to wait until you are alone in life to find this out, but it's better than never finding out. And it will give meaning to the rest of your life.

For instance, take my dog and cat. Part of me agreed with those who said I was tied down. Another part of me enjoyed my pets' company. So—facing the fact that my dog was getting on in years, would I get another dog if he died?

Earlier in my life, I wouldn't have anticipated the

decision, simply because I didn't think in terms of making choices. If I had a pet, I took good care of it. But did I *choose* to have one? Or two? And if so, why? Now that the choice was mine, I had to answer those questions.

Well, one week I boarded my dog and cat for three days because I had to be away from home frequently during that time. Frankly, I liked being released from my responsibilities. I could do things on the spur of the moment without feeling guilty about not feeding my pets at the usual time. My friends enjoyed it, too, because I was more at their disposal. I could also attend meetings without concern about how long they lasted. At night I certainly noticed the absence of affectionate, demanding companions, but I didn't feel lonely. I felt something else: a preference I had never noticed before. *I actually like taking care of a creature I love. I actually like being responsible to that creature, of whom I also ask a lot in terms of good company and protection. The act of caring warms me.* I discovered that I like a methodical life that runs according to schedule. I prefer eating three times a day and at certain hours. I always have, although I always gave way to other people's preferences. I still do—but I only have to do it some of the time, and that is what I choose. I can accommodate other people's irregularities as long as my life is regular. That's simply the kind of person I am.

I have a friend who is exactly the opposite. Beverly would love to have a dog, but she knows it wouldn't be fair to herself or the animal. She's hardly ever home.

She leads a very busy life teaching and administering a number of professional organizations.

That's her preference, and it colors her life. She likes to feast on one meal a day and she is bored with regularity. Fine—as long as she understands her needs and sees to it that they are satisfied. We get along very well, partly because each of us sees to our own needs and accommodates the other's.

Being confronted with the task of pleasing myself has taught me many things. First of all, it's not a sin, nor is it selfish. It is essential to building a worthwhile life for yourself, not only if you are doing it alone, but even if you choose to share your life with another person. The identity you discover in yourself is something you will be able to bring into your most important relationships.

What I find particularly interesting is that as I begin to understand who I am, I can remember more of my earliest years in this world. This is something many women I know have also experienced, usually after they have made some peace with being alone. My experiences began with remembering the times I used to spend writing those clumsy little poems I mentioned earlier. For some reason I had forgotten them for years. Then, as I remembered, I realized that I had always wanted to write, which of course is what I had been doing for most of my professional life. But I never took my work seriously or considered it a vital part of myself. Writing was simply something I did. Actually it is something I must do, and I understand that now. I also like to live within range of a large city where I can get in touch with new and exciting ideas, but for my every-day life I require the relative serenity of some space and some trees. I would not function well in a totally remote area, however beautiful it might be. And, curiously, I knew those things long ago. I grew up on the fringes of a large metropolitan area, but when I am in the country, I feel as if I am home.

Finding the Future in the Past

Sara, recently widowed, is beginning to recall that as a child she often cried at the sight of dogwood blooming. Only dogwood? No. Anything beautiful makes her cry—now. Sara is realizing that she is more than a widow, more than alone; she is an artist. She always has been, but she pushed that part of herself aside because she thought it was frivolous, and there were weightier things for her to do. Her late husband was an illustrator and as Sara reminisces, "One artist in a family is enough." Now, however, there is another. Sara has become an excellent photographer—which is not to say, "Hooray! Here's a woman who has found her vocation!" Sara has been a social worker for most of her adult life. But expressing her creativity has brought more than pleasure and variety into her world. "Just knowing that a person can hold on to the beauty in life—and that's what I can do as an artist—gives me a lot more stamina when I'm dealing with something that's ugly. And in my work I often have to deal with things that are ugly."

A much younger woman, who was trying to plan

sensibly for her future, was frustrated when she didn't seem to fit into the business world. "I did all the right things," Diana said, "but they kept coming out wrong. I have a whole file of turndowns from personnel departments, and when I finally got a job, I hated it. But I stuck it out because my parents had given up so much for my education, and they were worried about things like security. Security—that's a joke! I worked nights as a waitress to help pay my rent for a tiny apartment in a city where I didn't know anyone."

Diana was a popular waitress, especially with children. They used to dash ahead of their parents to sit at one of her tables—and to be hugged and lifted up into the air on their way to the salad bar. Diana enjoyed children immensely, and the joy was reciprocated.

"When I went home at night, I felt better just thinking about those kids," Diana said. "Then I began to remember that I had always liked taking care of children. I understood how they felt about being little and wanting to be big. I could talk to them better than I could talk to people in my office. I don't know why I didn't think of it before, but I really was cut out to be a teacher." Diana is back in school now, working toward a degree in education. Her parents weren't exactly happy about it at first. They know how deeply Diana cares about people, and they're afraid she'll be hurt when she can't do as much for them as she wants to do. But they're beginning to come around. There are worse things in life than being hurt.

Yes, there are. And one of them is to be a type rather than a whole person. Or to avoid life rather than struggle with it. Or to smother the energy God has created in us with a woolly security blanket.

Why do we forget these clues to our identity? Why do parts of ourselves have to wait so long to fit into our lives? Once we claim them, we wonder how we ever felt complete without them. And the answer is: we didn't. Something was always missing. Even when we had what we thought we wanted.

We didn't have ourselves. We didn't think we could—without hurting or even giving up some of the people we loved.

I'd Like to Be Me—But . . .

Frances is a widow in her early sixties. She lives alone but has a lot of friends, two married children, and a few grandchildren who visit her often. She doesn't like to spend much time by herself, but every now and then she feels the need for her own company. "I usually do what other people want to do. I go where they want to go. That's fine with me—except for sometimes. Then I want to spend a day by myself, with no one else around, just puttering around my apartment, singing to myself. I'd never sing in front of anybody! I go for a swim at the Y before dinner. I cook something fancy, just for me. And I have a good time."

Recently Frances was ready for one of those "good times." But she had already agreed to spend the day at her son's home. "I don't know what came over me," she told me, "but I was such poor company. I didn't feel like talking, although I tried. I didn't want to go out to eat—and we went to such a nice restaurant. I wasn't interested in anything we did, but I tried not to show it. All I wanted to do was be home, by myself. And I felt so guilty about it."

I understood what she meant. I recalled the way I decided to spend Christmas Day a few years ago. Ordinarily I invite friends to spend the day with me or I visit them, both of which I enjoy. But that particular year I wanted to spend Christmas alone. I had always wanted to, at least once.

I relish the rituals of the Christmas season. I like the hurried shopping and the intricate preparations. Like so many people, I take on too much, begin too late, and end up exhausted. The one moment of meaning always came at a Christmas Eve church service, where I could sit quietly, reaching for God's hand and waiting for Christmas to become part of me. It never lasted long enough. No matter how hard I tried to hold on to that nearness of God's love, I always lost some of it in the bustle of fussing too much, eating too much, and picking up so much paper and ribbons from gifts pleasurably opened.

So I decided to spend one Christmas Day exactly as I pleased. My friends were puzzled. They thought I might be getting depressed, but my enthusiasm convinced them that I wasn't. Nevertheless they kept calling me right up through Christmas morning, telling me that I was welcome to spend the day with them. At the last minute I almost gave in—because I began to look at myself as I thought they saw me: a little odd. Perhaps a little offending, because I didn't want to be with people who loved me. Besides, I might get lonely.

But I held out. And I spent the most wonderful Christmas of my life. I went for a long walk with my dog. I played woolly-ball with my cat. I sang carols, thanked God right out loud for my blessings, ate a very good dinner, read through all my cards by the light of my Christmas tree—and just allowed myself to feel God's love for the world. I can still feel it. I bring it with me now when I visit friends on Christmas Day.

What Do You Do with the Pain?

Discovering your identity will have its effect on those you love. Expressing your feelings can be inconvenient, uncomfortable, and downright threatening. Acting on what you feel may bring strong reactions in return. They may be temporary. They may last. They may end what you believed to be a relationship.

Is it worth the risk? The pain?

The same questions must have been asked by Christ's followers, who had to decide whether or not to follow His advice to go out into the world. To meet the demands life would make on them. To flinch under its unfairness. To rejoice in its sweetness. To expose their sensitivity to its callousness. To be lifted up by its clumsy gentleness. To be challenged by its incredible possibilities. To realize how much love was needed there.

Why would anyone want to take such a chance? Why would anyone want to give up even the most unrewarding role for such an uncertain venture?

It's easy for us to assume that those men and women had nothing better to do. That they had nothing to lose by seeking their created selves. But in reality they were very much like us. Some were alone, some were in families, couples, groups. All of them had relationships they surely didn't want to give up. And all of them must have been troubled by what might happen if they could no longer please their friends and loved ones. If they could no longer hold on to the approval that brought them closeness.

Some took the risk. Some didn't. Each of us has to make our own choice. God will not make it for us.

It is especially difficult to risk a relationship when one is alone. We count on friends, family, loved ones to give us the feeling that we belong, to keep us from believing that we are unwanted. Losing the closeness of even one person is painful, and very good reason for us to wish we had never begun our search for wholeness.

If someone rejects the person you have become, you will know pain that is deep, long, and sharp, the kind that screams in your ears. And you can hold your hands over your ears, but you won't drown out the pain. It is trying to destroy what you have become, and you will realize that. You will want, for a time, to return to what you were, to play the part, to do what is expected—anything to be close again. And yet you will know that such a return is impossible for you. If you have been a whole person for even a moment, you can never again be less than that. Because you have experienced the unique communication that is possible only between you and the One who created you. You have discovered how much love went into the making of you and how much value you have. You'll find you can't give that up. You won't.

Rejection is painful on both sides. I know Sylvia's parents very well, and I have known her since she was an infant. Her parents object to her independence. They don't understand why she can't live at home. They are concerned about her safety—"She comes home at night, sometimes, and you know how apartment buildings are. Nobody cares what goes on." They wish she could find "a nice young man—someone who could take care of her." They don't like her friends—"All they care about is having a good time." They feel neglected—"She hardly ever comes to see us—and she lives just a few blocks away."

Sylvia feels as if she lives worlds away. She has an interesting, responsible job for someone so young—because her talent is outstanding. She designs hotel lobbies and travels all over the world. "I don't think my family even knows what I do," she says. "They never ask me about my work—yet that's the biggest part of my life. Sometimes, when I've done something I'm very proud of, I want to pick up the phone and tell my mom and dad. But I don't—not anymore. They'd listen and say something like, 'That's nice, dear.' Know what I mean? Now—if I called them up and told them I was dating some terrific guy, they'd pay attention!"

I was reminded of some of the people I know. They are well-meaning, caring people who would love to see me happy, but according to what *they* mean by happy. If

I'm working on a book, they aren't interested. If I'm improving my house, they change the subject. If I just came back from a trip, they never ask where I've been. All they want to know is, "Are you dating anyone?" That, to them, would be an assurance that I was going to be all right. I can respect that—but the fact that they don't understand what is "all right" for me does hurt. It prevents a relationship by imposing an identity on me that isn't mine.

How do you make the pain of rejection go away?

Not by pretending it isn't there, because that isn't possible. It will show in your face, slow your steps, sound in your breathing. Not by passing it on to someone else through impatience, anger, resentment, envy. Now that you can feel what others feel, you will only increase your own suffering.

You will have to live with your pain for a while. Until you can begin to realize that you are worth the price you paid. Until you can begin to use and count on your ability to get along in the world, to make a life for yourself. Until the love you feel coming into you makes it possible for you to build real relationships.

You may not notice it right away, but the pain will begin to end. As your ability to love enables you to touch other lives without surrendering your own, you will notice a difference in yourself. You will smile again. You will have energy. You will be healed. The pain will be gone. It won't come back again—except, occasionally, as a brief, sad memory of someone you almost can't remember being.

5

A FRIEND IS MORE THAN

ONE PERSON

I WAS DIFFERENT before I was alone. So were my friends. Some of them have survived my transition. Some of them haven't, and I grieve for the loss.

A friend of mine resents the way she is treated by some of the people who knew her when she was married. "They never invite me to their homes anymore," Linda says. "It's always lunch at some restaurant—and always with the woman. I don't even get to see my friends' children!"

"You're lucky," Marion tells her. "Since Ken died, no one wants to see me—even for lunch. No one calls. You'd think I never had a friend in the world."

"I have friends," a young single woman says, half-smiling. "When they don't have anything else to do."

Being a friend when you are alone is not the same as being a friend when you are part of a couple, a group, or a family. Trying to duplicate what you had, even with the same persons, will break your heart. Exploring the one-on-one friendship isn't easy, but it has its rewards. One of them is that it permits—no, depends upon—a regard for individual differences.

Some of the friends who knew me before tell me,

"You're so different now," and they don't mean it in criticism. "I know you so much better," they add, which relieves me greatly. The fact is, I know myself better and so I am better able to make myself known. I guess you could say I'm more comfortable with the person I am, and that makes some people more comfortable with me. It makes some people more *uncom*-fortable, but that's another story.

I look for this same openness in the friends I make—and this may be why so few old friends can survive the upheaval in another friend's life. Because they are parts of a larger whole, a group, they may not identify with others as individuals. They look for similarities, for things that promise to bring them close. They are more likely to sweep any differences under the rug, and there the incompatible particles form lumps that trip us up. No, differences don't have to be resolved or made smooth, but they must be respected.

Who Your Friends Are

Friends have become more important to me now. Not because they take up my time or keep me from realizing that I am alone. They fill deeper needs, and I have learned what my needs are. So my reasons for being a friend are different, too. I realize that nobody has to put up with me because I am associated with a group or with a more pleasing person. Neither do I have to put up with someone just because that person happens to be here. A friend—my friend or the friend I am—has to give sustenance to life.

While I don't believe there is a perfect friend, I know there can be a perfect friendship. Mine is made up of a community of friends, no one of whom can give me everything I need. But each has some qualities that are vital to my life. For instance, I have a friend who appreciates my creative ideas, but gets nervous when I mention a problem. That's all right—I don't seek her company when I have problems. But when I tell her about an idea I just got, she not only understands it immediately but helps to build on it. Another friend enjoys sharing dinner and an evening at the theater with me. We can disagree about the play we saw and still enjoy discussing it; she has no interest in hearing about my dog and cat. I have another friend I can call on when my spirits are low and I'll scream if anyone tries to cheer me up. This is the kind of friend who cries when I cry because he feels what I feel—a rare gift, and I hope I return it. I have another friend who talks endlessly about the most meaningless things, but when I want to remind myself that there is goodness in this world, I will go to her.

For my part, I have learned that I can't be everything to a friend. I can only try to give what that person needs most at a particular moment and hope she or he will put up with the rest of me. I'm a good listener to one friend who doesn't want my advice, only my attention. She likes to make her own decisions, but it helps her to put her feelings into words that another person understands. Fine with me, although I have to resist the urge to tell her what to do with her life. With another friend I express my opinions easily, and that's what she wants. We don't think alike, and she wants to consider both sides of an issue before she makes up her mind. It works well for both of us, except for the times we try a little too hard to change each other's mind. Then, out of respect for each other's differences, we have to put a little distance between our conversations.

Don't Be Afraid to Disagree

In case it seems as if I choose my friends strictly for their compatibility—I don't. We don't simply exchange what is agreeable to us and forget about the rest. We have some difficult times. Our relationships are strained, sometimes to the breaking point. But if we can survive those times when our identities come into conflict, we have a stronger, more enduring friendship.

Some years ago I made the mistake of serving as an editor for a friend who was writing an excellent book. We had no problems with the book. The company I worked for wanted very much to publish it. But when my friend and I got down to negotiating a contract, we discovered it was not the same as discussing different opinions. We had totally different interests, and we were determined to defend them. I was concerned with publishing costs and the need to make a reasonable profit. My friend was concerned with the time and creative effort that go into writing a book and her need to live while she was doing it. They were normal points of conflict in a business negotiation—but not in a friendship. We felt as if we were attacking each other;

as friends we had been supportive, not competitive. Each of us blamed the other for putting business first and friendship second—which is exactly what we *should* have been doing. Each of us felt that the other should give in—because, well, we were friends. It was the same as saying, "If you really care for me, you'll give me what I want"—an attitude that is as bad for friendship as it is for business.

That was when my friend and I realized that we really didn't like everything about each other. We could admire each other's conviction—from a distance. Up close it was uncomfortable. We counted on each other's sensitivity; we always knew when the other was hurt. But we didn't like causing the pain.

We had to make a decision. Would we give up negotiating a contract or give up our friendship?

We didn't give up anything. But we did grow up a little. We realized that we were the same persons in friendship and in business, but that we expressed ourselves differently because the situations were different. We learned why an identity is never the same from one moment to the next—that is, as long as we are reacting honestly to life.

We did manage to compromise on a fair contract. We are also very good friends to this day. Occasionally we do some business with each other, although we know now that at such times we will not always like what we see in each other. Nevertheless, knowing more about each other has made it possible for us to have a stronger relationship—one that is able to include closeness, distance, compatibility, conflict, admiration, and even distaste. Those are the things you get with a whole person.

How Does a Relationship Happen?

A relationship is a clearing where two—or more—people can replenish themselves after the world wears them down. Where they can find release from the noise, distractions, and contradictions they encounter in other areas of their lives. Where they can work on their dreams, repairing some of the damage that has been done to them, making them more world-worthy for another try at fulfillment.

More important, a relationship is where the love in each of us can make contact with the love that is part of another created person. It is the next best thing to being in touch with God. It can—*should*—remind us who we are.

A relationship requires two or more whole persons who are willing to become real to each other. And that takes time.

We need to be interested. We have to be willing to explore each other's character, features, thoughts, sensitivities, weaknesses, strengths, values. Not to like or dislike, but to make contact. To invite each other into the clearing that a relationship occupies in this world. To be patient if the invitation is not immediately accepted and acted upon. To—gently, without crowding—step closer, perhaps beyond the halfway point. But, out of regard, no more than that. Not to insist upon knowing, or upon knowing instantly; not to thrust one's own identity up front to show how it should be done; but to make it apparent that the knowing of the other is very earnestly sought.

We need to be inquisitive. Not prying. Or probing. But wanting to know more than just the available facts about a person. Wanting to go where the eye cannot see and the ear cannot hear. How does this other person feel? About everything? Such things are important to us. Not because we are trying to find similarities to ourselves. But, rather, because we are open to differences and distinctions. Not because we want to possess what the other person is or has. But because we want to observe the coming together of a whole person—mind, body, and soul—in its own time, its own way. We want to accept the other as a work in progress—not as something complete—that may change, be less or more or different as time goes on.

We need to be perceived. Now it is our turn to be known. Without apology or exaggeration. Without asking for acceptance. But with the courage to allow another person to know us as well as we know ourselves. More than that—with an eagerness to be known.

We need to interact. Finally, we come to what many of us are seeking in a relationship: the acknowledgment of each other's existence and the caring about each other's well-being. But it often eludes us. Because we can't possibly acknowledge and care about someone unless we know who that person is, and who we are.

It was our not knowing that put Christ on the cross in full view of our horrified eyes. It is our not knowing that makes it possible for us to hurt, even destroy, each other.

Unless I know you well enough to experience what you think and feel, then you aren't real to me. You aren't flesh, blood, and frailty. I can't hear you cry out in need or sing for joy. Your anticipation and contentment mean nothing to me, because I don't realize you have such feelings. I have never allowed you to express them to me. I speak at you, not to you. I can't meet your eyes or allow you to look into mine. So I am not chilled by your fear and disappointment. I can't weep over your sorrow—or stretch out my own faith to help you endure it.

I can strike you and not hold myself responsible for the pain I cause. I can hammer nails into your hands and not hear the sharp intake of your breath. I can thrust a spear into your side and say it didn't hurt.

Perhaps that is why we are so quick to affix labels on people. Or to categorize them into types. It prevents our knowing them, prevents us from feeling responsible for what happens to them.

Negotiating a Friendship

Because a one-on-one friendship is so vital to the life of a person who is alone, it has to be negotiated with some care. How, for instance, can two people learn to be comfortable in a relationship that includes both what they like and don't like about each other?

How did Christ—who certainly was alone—form deep, lasting friendships with so many imperfect people? One of them could sit up all night with Him, talking about religion and the heart of man—but always in secret. One was brave enough to admit he was a coward—but he also was an embezzler. One was a generous host—but only for the right people. One was devoted—but always trying to tell Him what to do. One was efficient—but cranky under pressure. One was compassionate—but possessive. One was steady—but slow to decide.

And there were many others. How were *they* able to share a friendship with a Man they didn't always understand? A Man who could be concerned about feeding strangers, yet could ask His friends to risk their lives for Him? A Man whose compassion for the helpless drove Him to attack profiteers, yet turned His thoughts to His suffering mother even while He was nailed to a cross? A Man who truly enjoyed their company, yet could leave them?

It is very difficult for any two people to have a relationship while their identities are still forming—which is the point at which most of us are. We need to know more—about ourselves and about each other—and the best way to get that information is from our relationship with God. Not by asking questions and getting answers. God doesn't work that way. He describes us by loving us. By understanding us. And as we respond to that love and understanding, we begin to realize that we, too, have those capacities within ourselves. We, too, can love and understand another. We can be a friend.

I have not always had a friendship with God. In fact,

I turned to Him only when I seemed to run out of other possibilities.

I have always wanted to be a good friend. I was drawn to many people. I tried in every way I knew to make myself helpful to them. Their problems became my problems. I almost welcomed a crisis in their lives because it gave me a chance to be important to them. And when their problems were solved, with or without my help, I felt a little left out. Maybe they didn't need me anymore?

And so I went from one friend's crisis to another's—until I had one of my own. There were offers of help; I was not abandoned. But I didn't know how to make use of that help because I had no idea what my needs were. Only one suggestion appealed to me: a friend with a small apartment in New York invited me to come and stay there. "Let me give you some emotional chicken soup," she said. "I have to go away in a few days, but while I'm here, we can talk. Then you can have the place to yourself. It might be good for you."

I knew that when she said "we can talk," she meant that she would listen. Because she is that kind of a friend. But the most attractive part of her offer was the solitude. I *wanted* to be alone, although I didn't know why.

I left as soon as I could pack. And for two days I talked. And slept. And talked. And slept. I can't remember my friend saying anything, although I'm sure she did. I can't even remember what I said. But I remember the kindness, the gentleness in my friend's eyes. They spoke for her.

91

Then I was alone. In a large city. Every morning I got up, dressed, and went out. I walked in several different directions. And I noticed that there were so many other people who seemed to be alone—until they stopped to speak to someone. I would see them laughing, heads thrown back. Or stooped to listen more attentively to a serious matter. Or waving across the street, shouting something I couldn't hear, but bringing a smile to someone's face.

I would stop to buy food and bring it back to prepare. I wasn't ready to eat in a restaurant, and, besides, it was cheaper to cook. But the first laugh I had was on myself. I noticed that no matter what went wrong in my life, I automatically ate three times a day. Not as much as I usually ate, but the need was apparent. As I have mentioned before, I am a methodical person—not a beguiling trait, to be sure, but one that still means a lot to me because it was the beginning of my awareness that I was a person. I had *a* characteristic—something that was not going to go away.

Gradually I began to realize that even in a city as large as New York, there are neighborhoods, where people know and recognize each other. And some of the people in my friend's neighborhood were beginning to know me by sight. They nodded as we passed. The world is not an unfriendly place—if you allow it enough time to make your acquaintance. Which I was very willing to do, except that I had to make my own acquaintance first.

I was becoming aware that I didn't know how to be a friend. I had been a rescuer, a burden-bearer, a confidante—but those are some of the things a friend does, not what a friendship is. Something was missing, some quality that could speak without words, if necessary—like my friend's gentle eyes, or the wave of a hand, or a head bent in concern or arched back in laughter—to say that I cared.

I wanted someone else to experience the love that I was beginning to feel coming my way—from God. He was there. His presence was making me aware of myself. Our friendship was beginning.

Each one of us is very real to God. But we have trouble allowing Him to become real to us. We know what we have done to Him. We know it can happen again. And again. We don't want to feel His hurt. It may be more than we can bear. But if we allow God to become real to us, we will discover that He is trying to make us aware of our ability to love. To care. To look after. These are the best parts of ourselves.

How, then, do we find out what kind of a Person God is? By letting Him love us.

I began to understand that our relationship with others begins with our relationship with God. From the moment I began to know Him as a Friend, I began to be a friend. To Him. To myself. To others. I became willing to be known because I was someone God loved.

Friendship is more than what we do for each other or say to each other. More than the time we spend together, which may not be very much. It is a commitment to each other of certain qualities that each of us has—and may not have used before. So, by being each other's friend, we discover more of our identity.

Friendship is patience. Each of us is growing into a whole person. That takes time. Don't try to live my life for me, and I won't try to live yours. I may be too quick to make a decision, and you may be too slow, but let's not try to change each other. Let's give ourselves the opportunity—as God does—to learn from our mistakes. But—as God does—let's reach out a hand if one of us starts to fall.

Friendship is compassion. It hurts to learn, so let's not compare our aches to see whose is greater. Let our individual pain teach us what the other is feeling. It will lessen our suffering.

Friendship is sovereignty. Each of us has a life that is uniquely our own. I know you have hopes for me. And there are things I wish you could accomplish—because you have it in you to do them. But let us keep our dreams to ourselves. Don't ask me to live up to your expectations. Help me to live up to mine.

Friendship is mercy. We won't always be proud of each other. There will be times when we would rather not know each other. But let's try to remember what each other really is—especially when we aren't that way.

Friendship is being there. I may not always understand you. I may not always approve of what you do. But I won't leave you. Even if you ask me to.

Will you be there for me? Can we be the kind of friends to each other that God is to us?

6

THE FAMILY YOU CREATE

ONE OF THE THINGS I learned when my aloneness made it necessary for me to grow up is that part of me will always be a child. No, that's not a contradiction. It's true of us all. The creative part of us, the ability to form mental pictures of things not yet seen, an idea coming into one's consciousness—that is the child in us. Laughter, tears, my being able to feel what you feel without your telling me—that is the child in each of us. It isn't an age. It's a sensitivity. A quality that should remain a part of us. But one that should never get in the way of our growing up.

Maturity is not the destruction of the child in us. Quite the opposite. Maturity is allowing—encouraging—the adult part of ourselves to become strong enough to protect the sensitivity of the child.

The trouble is, most of us don't like being an adult. It hurts. It's demanding. It's so serious, uncomfortable, not always popular. Do we *have* to?

No. We can allow the child to meet life for us. To rush forward with arms outstretched—trusting, affectionate, full of the certainty that everybody loves everybody and everything is going to be all right. We can watch the asking eyes turn sad as promises are made and not kept. As gifts are offered with conditions attached. When there is too little time and not enough attention. When affection is withdrawn as quickly as it was given. When lies are discovered and there is no remorse for them. When words are spoken in loud, angry voices.

And we can watch that child take a blow on the cheek and fall back, too stunned for tears. Someone must have made a mistake. She meant no harm. She is only a child.

We can watch her reach out again, this time with some hesitation. We can see her grasp a hand that pulls away and strikes another blow.

We can watch the child lose all ability to love, to trust, to hope, to engage this world. We can see suspicion and fear come into her eyes. She will keep her distance from certain kinds of people. Perhaps from all people. And she will think that something is wrong with her.

Inside each of us is a child who has been wounded to some degree from trying to cope with the world. If we are fortunate, we carry only a few scratches. But some of us are severely battered, because the child in us has been sent to do what the adult in us would rather not. And the child can't. It is not equipped to make our decisions and solve our problems. It cannot handle disappointment, deceit, unkindness, brutality, oppression, frustration, hate. Our adult can. Not easily. But effectively. Not without getting hurt. But our adult can recover from hurt better than our child can. It has more strength. More smarts. And the ability to understand that the world is not a playground where everyone is out to have fun. The adult in us can bind its own wounds—and those of the child.

It isn't fun to be an adult. But it is reassuring. We don't have to hide from life. From relationships, from fulfillment or from love. As adults, we can handle them.

Act Your Age

Yet the child must be cared for—and who is going to do that? If you have outlived your parents, or if your parents need more care than they can give to you, what do you do when the child in you needs a mother and father? If you deny the child, the other areas of your life will suffer for it.

Sometimes I can serve as the parent my child needs. If I am working too hard and too long, if I am suddenly aware that the child in me needs to play a little, I can provide for that. And it does me good. The crankiness that was creeping up on me begins to disappear. Sometimes a feeling of "Oh, what's the use!" turns out to be nothing more than a child who was told to sit still too long.

I can be both mother and father to my child, just as God is both to me. I can offer a fatherlike counsel and support if the world seems a little too awesome to the child. I can comfort the child and let her know that she is not alone in the dark. I can also tell her, in a loving way, when she is carrying on too much and must let me be.

There are times when I don't want to cry in front of

someone. When I want to make my point without emotion. When I want to make a decision based on reason, fairness, and an awareness of the facts. When I must speak from authority rather than sentiment. When I must concentrate on what is going on rather than what ought to be. When I want to be taken seriously.

Like many women, I cringe when someone claims that a woman is too emotional to handle responsibility. And I still hear such claims. But I cringe even more when I remember that for a good part of my life I was guilty as charged. Not, however, because I was incompetent, but because I didn't ask the little girl in me to step aside and let the adult take over. Men have been encouraged to do that since they were little boys, and now *they* have a problem: letting those little boys back into their lives. We seem to need all there is of us—but not always at the same time and in the same place.

A Family in Spirit

But while I can be both mother and father to my child, I can't give the child part of me—or even the adult—everything it needs. I can't heal all the hurts. It is hard to cry on my own shoulder. I run out of encouragement. I need pep talks. I need the family I don't have anymore.

One of my friends seems to understand that, without my saying a word. She has an uncanny sense of timing, and at just the right moment I receive a package from her. Inside is a beautiful afghan—

hand-crocheted and in my favorite colors. I have one on my bed, one in my car for cold mornings, one for my lap when I sit up reading. "There's love in every stitch," she wrote on the card enclosed with the first one. I believe it. I have felt it when I pull them around me. There is no disappointment, no harsh word, no bruised knee that can't be healed by their warmth. They are my heirlooms. I feel as if they have been passed down to me by someone who has been where I am going, someone who understands how it feels. They are my place to cry—and my place to find a reason to go on and try again. I feel as if I have been comforted by a mother.

I wasn't always able to get what a child needs from my family. I think this is true of many families; they do the best they can, but the demands on them are greater than they can meet. And the various family members, like me, go their disappointed ways, doing without the care they should have. Is there any one of us who doesn't at times need to be consoled, even pampered, emotionally held close and rocked back and forth, given a glass of milk and a plate of cookies at a kitchen table close to a stove smelling of good things cooking? Don't we all need to be reassured that everything will be all right in a little while? Don't we all need to be told that we are good children, loved and wanted children? Those needs don't stop when we grow up—or when a family is disrupted.

I think it was God being both father and mother to me that made me realize that I had to seek parent relationships with other human beings. In effect, I had to re-create a sustaining family, not necessarily patterned after my own, but one that would nevertheless give to me what everyone needs from a family—a sense of continuity because you know others have gone before you and others will follow, a source of wisdom gained from struggles you have yet to go through, a recognition of your own worth in this world, and a generosity that is able to make room for you in the hearts of others.

In my original family I was an only child. Now, in my sustaining family, I have several brothers and sisters, not all of them with the same last name. I have more than one father, more than one mother. One of my fathers is a teacher, one a retired editor, one was a farmer with an exceptional ability to bring life out of tired soil. One of my mothers is a wife and mother whose talents are evident in the lives of her family. Another was a fairly hard-nosed businesswoman, until you got to know her better. My brothers and sisters come in many ages and sizes. I even have the good fortune to feel a grandmotherly relationship to some of the younger persons in my re-created family. I don't address my relatives by family names, and most of them don't even know they have been adopted by me. We are simply important to each other and we care about what is happening in each other's lives. We may not see each other often and we don't always spend holidays together, but when I need the belonging that only a family can give to me, I know where to go. The child—and the adult—in me are well cared for.

And is that the end of the story? Do we all come

together as whole persons and live happily ever after?

We do not. Because even if we have found our identity, that identity will express itself differently in each relationship. We will not always be seen as whole persons, but rather as providers of what someone else needs.

How much of ourselves can we afford to give? And to how many different people?

Where Do You Fit in a Group?

After being on our own for a while, it can be absolutely knee-wobbling to be welcomed into other lives. To be one of the group. To be understood, to share the same humor, the same angers, the same pleasures. It can turn back the clock in the sense that we feel as if we are held warm and close again. Safe.

Until it becomes apparent that we couldn't possibly know very much about each other on such short acquaintance. And as we learn more about our identities, we feel a twinge of alarm: There will be points of conflict. The rough edges are still there.

For a moment we are tempted to conceal them. To offer only the parts of ourselves that give us a sense of belonging. But we can't. Not anymore. We have lived in our own skins too long. We recognize an image when we see one.

Do we have to abandon a relationship that engages only part of us? Can an individual be comfortable in a group?

In His human experience, Christ came up against

the same questions. He had a very large spiritual family, and almost all of them wanted to keep Him to themselves. For a very simple reason: He had something they needed, something that enabled them to become more complete human beings. He was company for the lonely. Courage for the fearful. Motivation for the confused. Direction for the lost. Understanding for the neglected. Truth for the deceived. Energy for the exhausted.

Christ had other qualities as well: dedication, persistence, responsibility, forthrightness, stubbornness, impatience, endurance, acceptance, reliability, awareness, among others. Useful? Yes. Needed? Yes. But not particularly desired. Couldn't He leave them out of His relationships?

He couldn't. And neither can we.

Christ can be a father to you, a mother to me, a child to someone else, all at the same time—because He does not allow us to possess Him. We don't have to accept all of Him—but He does accept Himself. Our relationship with Him may be limited to what He can give us at a particular moment, but everything else that He has is there if we need it.

There is a difference between need and possession.

Need is an honest reaching out for help. It is somewhat tunnel-visioned in that it can see only what it requires to get on with life. It uses well whatever it receives, and very often the need is ended. Until another kind of need is realized—and another source of help can then be found. A real need can be a pest, but never a threat to our identity. It will leave without hard feelings if we don't have what it wants.

Possession is different.

Possession is manipulative. It appears to be a need, but it is much more than that. It not only wants what we can give, but wants it exclusively. It sees that there is more to us, but rejects what it does not want. More than that, it tries to destroy what it does not want. It ridicules, accuses, claims injury, casts doubt. Possession can make us feel that the only part of us that is worthwhile is the part we give to it. And we are called upon to give endlessly, because possession consumes what it needs, but doesn't give it back to the world.

For a long time I tried to negotiate a relationship with a woman who saw me not only as a mother but as a father. She was middle-aged, reluctantly divorced, and unsure of herself. She had never worked in her life and she needed a job desperately, a need that introduced us to each other through a mutual friend who thought I might be able to help.

I was sympathetic with Donna's predicament. It's very hard to sell yourself to an employer when you don't think you have anything to offer. I arranged for Donna to have some information interviews with friends in several different areas of business. All of them thought highly of her. She was intelligent, personable, and articulate. She also listened attentively to all the advice she was given—and then did absolutely nothing with it. She did not want to take a course—of any kind. She thought entry-level jobs were "demeaning." Part-time work didn't pay enough.

I was becoming impatient, but I felt guilty about it. I kept reminding myself that Donna was not prepared for the world she had to confront. It seemed unfair to ask her to be realistic when reality had never been part of her earlier life. Besides, whenever I tried to make Donna realize that she had very little choice in the matter of a job, she began to cry. She thought I was criticizing her. Eventually, so did I.

Until I began to understand that Donna wanted me to respond to her as if I were her consoling parent—and nothing else. My attempts to lift her spirits, my concern about her dwindling finances, my encouragement of her own strengths, were rejected. Not that she had to accept them; she may not have been ready for them. And they may not have been as useful as I though they were. But they were not evidence of my insensitivity— and that is the way Donna interpreted them. If I felt sorry for her, I was a good friend; if I saw a way she could help herself, I was an enemy. Donna, who saw herself as a poor, helpless little girl, wanted me to be her parents. And nothing else. Ever. I had to disagree.

You may not want all that I can give you. But I want you to take what you do need—as long as you don't confine me to whatever that need is. Allow me my flexibility. It's part of my identity.

We can, each of us, be partners in a relationship and members of a group without giving up ourselves. We don't have to ask anyone else to acknowledge who we are—as long as *we* know. As long as *we* reserve the right to be not what someone else applauds but what God created.

The value of a spiritual family is that we can enter in as a person with an identity. We don't have to play roles that are assigned to us according to the date of our birth. But neither do we have to be limited to giving a small part of ourselves. We are persons meeting the needs of other persons, and as long as we recognize what we have, we can give all we've got. And never give it up.

7

THE GIVE-AND-TAKE
OF FAITH

NOW THAT I've been on my own for a while and seem quite comfortable there, I'm beginning to hear this comment from some of the people who know me, although not very well: "It must be nice to do whatever you please and not have to answer to anyone but yourself."

I'm reminded of those who look at me with a certain yearning in their eyes and tell me, "It must be nice to be a writer and work whenever you're in the mood." They don't see my lamp glowing late at night when a page is being written over and over until it's right. They don't know, when they see me strolling with my dog along a park path in the middle of the day, that my mind may be working very hard at the same time. They don't keep track of the weekends I don't take off. They don't know that my work exerts an authority over my life just as surely as if I had to report to a supervisor in an office.

It's the same with being alone. I don't do as I please, whenever I please. I do have to answer to someone. We all do.

A Struggle for Authority

I used to think that someone with faith always said yes to God. I couldn't imagine anyone disagreeing with Him and still being acceptable to Him. Yet, if you are at all familiar with the Bible, you'll remember that it is filled with stories of people taking issue with God. One even wrestled with Him. And they didn't consider themselves lacking in faith. Apparently neither did God.

You probably also remember those obstreperous characters as men. But not all of them were.

Abraham's wife Sara was hardly a yes-person. Mary, the mother of Jesus, had her doubts about God's intrusion into her life. And Jesus came up against some pretty strong-minded women in Mary, Martha, Magdalene, and an unnamed woman at the well. There were others, all of them women who trusted God, and their faith was intense. Nevertheless, at times they thought their way was better than His, and they let Him know it.

I had it out with God a long time ago about who was going to run my life. He does—because I have discovered that He does it much better than I do. I still object, frequently and strenuously, and I still go my own way some of the time. Usually that's when I discover that the direction I felt from God wasn't a command from an authoritative father. It was a well-meant indication that something up ahead of me was better suited to my needs than something else. Now that has to come from Someone who knows me very well— better than I know myself. But it also has to come from Someone who wants to show me more about myself— when I already think I know it all.

When You Think You Can—Watch Out!

After I survived the initial terror of becoming independent, I ran into another hazard. I became too self-sufficient. It happens to many of us. We hold our breath the first few times we dare to please ourselves, and then, when the sky doesn't fall in, we get to like it. Too much. We decide that we don't have to do *anything* we don't want to do.

Actually there are a lot of things we don't have to do, if we do them only to win approval and acceptance. But there are a great many other things we may not want to do, yet should do—because we have the capacity to meet very real needs that should not be ignored. I don't think God is telling us to suffer when He gives us that nudge in the ribs. I think He's hoping we'll discover how much more we are worth.

There is nothing wrong with being dependent, as long as it is occasional and doesn't become a life-style. As long as it provides us with the means to stand on our own feet. But we don't always use dependency wisely. We make a habit of it. We push each other down instead of helping each other up. We attach strings to what we offer: *I'll give you this if you'll do that.* Dependency has become a dirty word because too often it leads to bondage—under the guise of love.

Breaking away from that bondage and becoming self-sufficient is a necessary step in our progress toward a full life. But self-sufficiency can be deceptive. It can look like independence—and sometimes only God can point out the difference to us.

Being self-sufficient means that we live by our own strengths, make use of our own resources—which no doubt took us a long time to discover.

It there anything wrong with that?

No. Not wrong. Just not enough. We're using our strengths, all right, but selectively. We're building a small world tailored to our own preferences and convenience. And we're avoiding other people's problems because we've got enough of our own.

Who can argue with that?

God can. Because He gave us a great deal more to put into this world—which is not ours, after all, but His.

Independence goes far beyond self-sufficiency. It uses everything we are, but it also reaches out to other people's resources. It brings discomfort, inconvenience, and bother into our lives. It also brings fulfillment—and the incredible inner crackle that tells us we are persons.

Independence is the absolute freedom to open ourselves to God's urging, to God's need for us—without fear of enslavement or bondage. It is the astonished realization that God has created us with more muscle, more sensitivity, more intelligence, and greater capacity to care than we ourselves can ever use—unless, of course, we give *of* ourselves to those who have honest need of our abundance.

Knowing who we are, knowing how much we have, we do not—any longer—have to fear that we will surrender our sovereignty. We can give generously and never be impoverished. But we will not—any longer—live as less than the persons we know ourselves to be.

Dependency means, *I need you.*

Self-sufficiency means, *I can get along without you.*

Independence means, *We're in this world together.*

We need them all.

Understandably, we do not reach eagerly for independence. From a distance we see only its demands. We prefer the cloister of self-sufficiency; it is not *that* far from a refuge. We keep to ourselves. We try to scale our needs down to a bare minimum, which we can then satisfy easily. Meanwhile God keeps reminding us how much more we are. And must become.

So the struggle goes on: our saying we don't want to, and God saying yes, but—

I see the struggle going on in the lives of two single-parent mothers of young children. Both are divorced, both work outside their homes, and both want to amount to something. Sheila is a secretary by day and attends law school at night. It's a grueling schedule. She sees her two preteen sons every other Sunday—if they show up. The rest of the time the boys live with their father and his new wife.

"I don't have time to be a good mother to my boys

now," Sheila says, and the words hurt because she misses her sons. "First things first. Right now I have to get my degree. Later, when I'm in practice, when I've got a few dollars to do things for my boys, then I'll be a mother again."

She knows, though, that *then* may never come. Or it may come too late. She chooses not to allow that probability to alter her plans. She chooses, also, not to be the confidante, the supervisor, the worrier, and the advocate of two children who mean very much to her. But in denying them admittance to these qualities, she cuts herself off from some of the best parts of herself. Sheila doesn't like herself very much.

Margaret's goals aren't as clear-cut as Sheila's, possibly because she has allowed some obstacles to get in the way of them. She's an office manager for a small firm, and she knows she has the ability to go on to something on an administrative level in a large corporation. She's even turned down a few offers of better pay because the jobs would have made more demands on her time. And time is important to Margaret. It allows her to keep in close touch with her son and daughter. She calls them at home after school, and if they aren't there, she finds out where they are. She plans interesting athletic activities for them in the hours between school's end and her homecoming. Her children don't even realize they are being supervised because Margaret involves their friends in the same activities.

She's at home most evenings, sometimes in the company of friends. And most evenings, her children are not there. Until, of course, the hour when they are told they *must* be in bed. "Everybody tells me to go out and have fun," Margaret says, "and I suppose they're right. But it's no fun for me to wonder what my kids are doing. Bobby's friends are starting to get curious about drugs—I know it, even though he doesn't tell me. But one of these days he's going to say something about it. And I want to be here when he's ready to talk. That's the way he is—and I have to respect that. I can't force myself into his confidence. I just have to be there when he wants to let me in."

Neither Margaret nor Sheila is at ease with her way of life. Each of them is aware that she is leaving something out. And each of them has struggled with God over what that something ought to be. The marks of the struggle are apparent.

Sheila is tired from working hard, from inching closer to a goal that is still far away. She makes it her business not to be home more than absolutely necessary. She doesn't like the quiet. She used to look forward to the every-other-Sunday with her sons. Now she looks for excuses when they cancel: They miss their friends, they feel like strangers to their mother.

Sheila feels like a stranger to herself, but she wants it that way. She's a sensitive, responsible woman capable of good relationships—except that she doesn't know that part of herself. She didn't find it because she gave up struggling with God. She makes her own rules. The question that bothers her is: Is she giving up more than she is going to get back? In satisfying her ambition, is she denying a very important part of herself—her need to love? Is self-sufficiency enough?

Margaret's struggle goes on. She'd like a better job and she could handle it. But she can live with that concern. "Right now there are too many other things for me to do," she says. She's not complaining. "I have to pay attention to the people in my life. It's the way I am." Margaret is aware that she has more than one compelling need in life. She has also made peace with the fact that she can't deny one part of herself to satisfy another. Independence is a balancing act.

As we become independent, we begin to realize that not all of our needs will lead us to a goal. Some of them will take us, by way of a detour, to a better understanding of ourselves.

It's Our Choice

When I am very busy, I don't like to talk on the phone. And the last thing in the world I want to talk about is another writer's manuscript when I am having trouble with my own. So, when I was under pressure of a deadline, I began turning on my telephone-answering machine even when I was sitting right next to the phone. That way I could ignore calls for as long as I wished—even for days. I was congratulating myself in my efficiency and my newly realized strong-mindedness when a call came in from a writer friend who often called me when she felt anxious. There was a note of distress in her voice on the recorded message in my machine, but I tried to ignore it. *I* was self-sufficient. *I* didn't have to knuckle under to an interruption. I went on working.

A short time later I stopped. "Okay," I asked myself, "just what kind of person are you going to be?" Because I suddenly realized that I had a choice in the matter. Of course, I knew God was urging me to call my friend, but I knew I didn't have to do it. God would still love me if I didn't, and I could still put up with myself. But I decided that I didn't like *being* a person who didn't respond to a friend's distress. It may have been a false alarm. My friend may have been overreacting. That wasn't the issue. Was I there or wasn't I? Did I care about her? Yes. Was I going to act on what I felt?

Yes.

I called my friend and woke her out of a sound sleep. She had, in the meantime, solved her problem, which was fine. But I was still glad I called. If I care, then I have to do something about it if I want to live like the person I discovered myself to be. I think that's all God was asking me to do—to be the person He and I knew I was.

Single-mindedness is an admirable characteristic; it can get us where we want to go. But it can also cut us off from the world.

I have known Robin since she was a child, and even then she wanted to be an actress. She has talent and training, but she's quick to tell you that they aren't enough. "You have to be there at the right moment," she says, "when lightning strikes. And it doesn't strike many of us."

For several years Robin made a career out of trying to "be there at the right moment." She'd drop anything to go to an audition, and occasionally she got a small part. But not often enough to make a living. She took temporary jobs with flexible hours and lived at home to cut expenses.

"For a long time I thought it was fun," she says. "I dressed the part. I wore anything that was free. I felt that was the way an actress ought to look."

That was several years ago. Robin isn't young enough to play an ingenue anymore. And she didn't make it big enough, while she was young enough, to land many character roles. "Something happened when I hit thirty," she told me. "I got tired of eating peanut butter, tired of hoping my parents wouldn't sell their house and move to the Sun Belt. My friends were getting on with their lives. I realized I was more than an actress. I'm a person. I need more out of life than just hope."

One day while Robin was filling in as a typist in an advertising agency, she was offered a full-time job. She took it. "I'm not crazy about this kind of work," she says, "but it gives me some of the things I need. I've got an apartment and a roommate, some fairly decent clothes. And I feel better not having my mom and dad put off their own plans because of me. I feel free."

But—what about her talent? Robin hasn't abandoned it. Her knowledge and love of the theater are important parts of herself, and she is using them in writing television scripts. She hasn't sold one yet, but she can write on her own time. "Besides," she says, "there's no age limit for a scriptwriter, so I can stay with this forever. And one of these days I may even make a living doing what I love."

When we find ourselves alone, we have to make a lot of decisions about what is right and what is wrong. We can't simply go along with the crowd or even with the group. It's *our* decision. There will be times when we may not want to do what we know is right, but the decision isn't that simple. There is a right and there is a wrong in the world, and we are free to ignore the difference between them if we choose. But if we *know* the difference and we don't act on it, then we are betraying the person we are. Our faith can show us who we are, but the way we live makes that identity real.

"I always said I'd never go out with a married man." The woman who told me that had lost her husband to another woman, and she knew how much it hurt. But after living alone for some time, she missed the company of a man. "Just someone to talk to and have dinner with," she used to say. "Nothing serious. I'm tired of talking to women all the time." She was being pursued by the husband of a woman she knew, and while his behavior appalled her, she couldn't bring herself to tell him not to call her again. "I can't be rude," she said.

One day, when the man called to try again, the woman wasn't feeling very good about the world and she thought, "Why not? What's so wrong about it?" She agreed to have dinner with him. "I knew it was going to be more than that, but I was tired of being Goody Two-Shoes," she said.

Two hours later she called the man at his office and

canceled the date. "I couldn't do it. I couldn't bring that kind of pain into someone's life. I felt as if I were betraying myself, not only his wife. I guess I *am* Goody Two-Shoes, like it or not."

Right or wrong isn't a matter of liking it or not. Who you are isn't a matter of doing whatever you choose whenever you please. It's deeper than that. It isn't enough for us to know that we are honest; we have to experience *being* honest when we have a choice whether or not to be. Caring about someone is a sentimental exercise until we find out what it means to put that person's needs before our own. We are only God's intentions until we allow those intentions to become part of our flesh, to shape what we do with what we think. It is our values that tell the world who we are. But we communicate our values through the way we live. No matter what our intentions may be, or what we really mean, what we do *is* what we are.

Do I Know You?

I have known one man for many years—and yet I don't know him. Because I don't know what he stands for. He can see all sides of any issue—which is something every one of us should try to do—but he never takes a stand. Never has an opinion. He finds it almost impossible to say no to anyone, yet by saying yes to all, he makes promises he can't keep. He means well, but can do harm because his meaning is subject to change. His point of view is different from one day to the next, depending upon what he has read or heard.

Another man I know is what you might call opinionated. He comes to conclusions. He makes decisions and acts on them. At times he does battle with the world—and doesn't always win. He is not always a comfortable person to be with, but I know where he stands and what is important to him. I know who he is because I know what his values are.

What are values? Are they beliefs? Opinions? Conclusions? Things we admire and believe are good? Points of view? Ethics? Morals? Rules?

Only partly.

Our values, if we have them, express our vision of what God intends our world to be, yet what it may never become in our lifetime. But this vision—our values—this understanding between God and us of what we are trying to achieve, is real to us. We live by it, even if no one else does. We will even die by—and for—it. It is a possibility in the mind of God, just as we once were. And, like us, it can become visible, tangible, audible. It is our knowing what the world can be that enables us to feel at home here. We are connected by God's love for both of us.

"At home," however, does not mean that our lives will be serene. We will come under attack, frequently and sometimes severely, because we choose not to live according to the way the world is now. We will not trade our hard-earned values for its trends.

This nay-saying to the world is our wilderness experience. And, like Christ's, it will cost us dearly. But it will give to us, as it gave to Him, the ability to hold on to the identity we have finally discovered—no matter how great the temptation to surrender it.

The world has not changed since it confronted Christ for forty days and nights. It calls the same things by different names. It appealed to Christ's appetite; it threatened Him with harm; it offered Him power. It takes a somewhat more contemporary approach to us. It appeals to our greed: *I'll give you whatever you want.* It threatens to cut off our special privileges: *I'll stop loving you, unless . . .* It offers us approval: *I'll make you the person I want you to be.*

We can only answer that our values gives us something more important: We have God in our lives; He asks nothing in return for His love: He has given us the power to be ourselves.

This struggle between what God created and what the world would like to change almost tore Christ apart. It will do the same to us, and we have to wonder if we are prepared for such a battle.

We aren't. But God is. And the only way we're going to get through the wilderness intact is to hold on to Him for all we are worth.

How You Lose—It's Important

When our values come under attack, when we have to defend not only them but ourselves, we won't always win. Nevertheless, we must always live like winners.

By that, I mean living with complete honesty, integrity, purpose, compassion, insight, and stubborn adherence to what we believe is right. Then, when the crunch comes, when we are opposed, even vilified, and must do battle—we must *do* battle. If we are overcome, pushed aside, made light of, or crushed underfoot, we will go down intact. We will have given up nothing along the way. We will have nothing to hide, nothing to be ashamed of. We can, rightfully and eagerly, go to God with the tears in our throat and covered with bruises, and be comforted. Healed, if healing is possible. We can be restored—intact. Our values in place.

And sometimes, it does happen—we *do* win!

At first it didn't seem that way to Betsy. She was a reporter on a small daily newspaper and was becoming very popular on her beat. People trusted her; she was known for hard work, honesty, and a painstaking attention to facts. Sometimes she passed up a story because she didn't have time to check it for accuracy and still meet her deadline. She could keep a confidence—and people told her things. Until she wrote an article about a city-run recreation center for the handicapped. Betsy had uncovered some financial irregularities.

To her surprise, the article was considered an attack on the community. "Muckraking!" one of the councilmen called it during a radio interview. An aide to the mayor protested "such unfairness" to the newspaper publisher. Readers wrote angry letters to the editor.

"Nobody on my beat would talk to me," Betsy told me. "It didn't matter that I wrote the truth. They could have checked the facts, but they didn't. They blamed me for giving the town a bad name."

For a while, Betsy thought about quitting her job. "I wasn't even sure my editor was on my side. He was supposed to write an editorial supporting my story, but he kept stalling. I think everyone just wanted me to disappear, and for a while I thought it was a good idea."

But Betsy stayed. She had to work especially hard to get her information, but she did it. "I wrote every story the same way I'd always written—carefully," she said. And gradually the respect returned.

"People forgot all about the recreation center," Betsy said. "Until, about a year later, a state senator running for office started a campaign to clean up abuses against the handicapped. All of a sudden, I was a heroine! All of a sudden it was okay to write the truth—about everything."

Betsy's with another newspaper now. In another town. But she's the same person. She lives like a winner.

8

NOW THAT YOU'RE
A PERSON

I USED TO THINK that if someone loved me, that made me lovable. It worked the other way around as well. If someone stopped loving me, I was devastated.

After my marriage ended, I carried a lot of bitterness around with me. Gradually I began putting my life together in new ways, and it was a good life. But the bitterness was still there. Forgiveness for the hurt was impossible. I knew that someday I would have to deal with that, but I had no idea how.

I had grown up in the era of self-discovery. I had heard all about the value of loving oneself, and the words made sense to me. It was supposed to be good for a person to have self-esteem. It was supposed to make other relationships better. In my head, I agreed. In my life—I couldn't be sure what the words meant.

All I knew was that when someone stopped loving me, I began hating that person. Why?

I found the answer to that question only after I was able to give myself what I used to ask others to give to me: care and responsibility. This is the kind of love

God has always given me, just as He gives it to you. I learned it from Him.

The Care and Loving of You

Will I die from the lack of love? I very well might, and in that terrible apprehension I very well might hate the person who deprived me of what I had no right to ask. Hate and fear are very close emotions.

Yes, I know now what love is, and I think I understand why Christ said it casts out fear. I have learned how to love through loving the self God has helped me to understand. I care for His created person. I take full responsibility for her. And the most remarkable fruit of that experience has been my growing awareness of an ability to love others in ways I never knew were possible. Those I love don't have to love me back. We can be distant from each other, even opposed to each other, and there is still a way I can love. Not by any determination to love, not because I think I must, but because I have discovered that I am a loving person. It is natural to me to love. It is to each of us.

We do not need the approval of others. Nor should we try to change their point of view. We have no right to demand that someone must understand us to earn our love. We can still love those who don't agree with the way we choose to live—because we choose to live lovingly.

I can still love the family and friends who wish my life had turned out differently. I can still love those who want me to take a direction that is different from the one I have chosen. I don't need to be understood as long as I understand myself, and God has helped me to do that.

Because I know who I am, I am better equipped to perceive who you are. And we are not the same. We don't need to be.

In Good Company

Now that you have your identity—what do you want with it? You bring it into the world. You bring your intelligence, your sensitivity, your talent and abilities, your past mistakes—and your future ones—your uncertainties, your fears, what you wish could be, what you wish hadn't been. They're part of you.

Don't be afraid of the world. It can't defeat you. It doesn't own you. It didn't create you. It can give you some anxious moments; it will try to reshape you; it is quite capable of hurting you, but it cannot steal from you. What you have, what God has given you, you will never lose. And the more of it that you give, the more identifiable you become, the better the world will be—because you are in it.

Don't be afraid to love. You don't have to wait for someone to discover you and make love possible. You already *do* love. It is part of your being. Love is the expression of all we have discovered ourselves to be. It is the way we make ourselves known.

Don't be afraid to go alone. Because you won't be. I'll go with you. Not all of the way. Not all of the time.

I don't expect you to take care of me. But I want your company. I'm not looking for perfection. I have to live with my mistakes—and yours, too. But I see in you what I'm finding in myself: the person that God loves. And I love you, too.

Sometimes we may need to lean on each other. Other times we will pull far apart from each other. Sometimes we will look around and see no one there. But even then we will not be alone. God is with us. He always has been. But the difference—now—is that we know it.